Mark Harrison

Grammar Spectrum 2

Pre-intermediate

Oxford University Press

OXFORD
UNIVERSITY PRESS
Great Clarendon Street, Oxford OX2 6DP

Oxford University Press is a department of the University of Oxford.
It furthers the University's objective of excellence in research, scholarship, and education by publishing worldwide in

Oxford New York

Auckland Cape Town Dar es Salaam Hong Kong Karachi
Kuala Lumpur Madrid Melbourne Mexico City Nairobi
New Delhi Shanghai Taipei Toronto

With offices in

Argentina Austria Brazil Chile Czech Republic France Greece
Guatemala Hungary Italy Japan Poland Portugal Singapore
South Korea Switzerland Thailand Turkey Ukraine Vietnam

OXFORD and OXFORD ENGLISH are registered trade marks of Oxford University Press in the UK and in certain other countries

First published 1995
2008 2007
20 19 18 17 16 15 14

ISBN-13: 978 0 19 431413 8 Without answers

Typeset by Wyvern Typesetting, Bristol

Printed in China

ACKNOWLEDGEMENT

Illustrated by: Ann Johns

Introduction

Grammar Spectrum 2 is for pre-intermediate students of English. It explains and practises the grammar that pre-intermediate students need to learn. It can be used for homework, and in class. This book is part of the *Grammar Spectrum* series of books; students can use the whole series to progress from an elementary to an intermediate level of English.

Using the book

When you have a particular grammar problem, you can look it up in the Contents at the front of the book, or in the Index at the back. You can then study the unit that deals with that problem. Or, you can work through the book from beginning to end.

Each unit begins with an explanation of the grammar point, and then it has a number of exercises for students to practise the grammar they have read about. Students can write their answers in the book, or on a separate piece of paper. When you have finished the exercises, you can check your answers with the help of your teacher.

Form tables at the back of the book (pages 94–97) give information on Present Simple forms, **-ing** forms, past participles, etc.

Finishing the book

When you have finished studying the whole book, you can do the Exit tests on pages 98 to 101. In the Exit tests, every question tests something from a unit with the same number. If you make a mistake, for example in question 30, you can look back to unit 30 and study that unit again.

Enjoy your studies, and remember, when you have finished *Grammar Spectrum 2*, you are then ready to go on to *Grammar Spectrum 3*.

Contents

1 Present Simple (I start)

1 We form the Present Simple in this way:

POSITIVE

I / You / We / They	**start** at eight o'clock.	
He / She / It	**starts** at eight o'clock.	

NEGATIVE

I / You / We / They	**do not** / **don't**	**start** at eight o'clock.
He / She / It	**does not** / **doesn't**	**start** at eight o'clock.

QUESTIONS

Do	I / you / we / they	**start** at 8?
Does	he / she / it	**start** at 8?

2 With **he/she/it** we add -**s** to most verbs:

walk → walks get → gets leave → leaves

But there are some exceptions:

- We add -**es** to verbs which end with -**sh**, -**ch**, -**ss** or -**o**:

  finish → finishes catch → catches
  do → does go → goes

- We change some verbs that end with -**y** in this way:

  cry → cries worry → worries
  study → studies

- But we add -**s** to verbs that end with -**ay**, -**ey**, -**oy** or -**uy**:

  pay → pays play → plays buy → buys

3 We use the Present Simple for facts:
*Secretaries **work** in offices.*
*Ruth **does** all her work very well.*
*It **doesn't snow** in this country.*

4 We use the Present Simple for repeated actions (e.g. habits, and events on a timetable):
*I usually **play** tennis at weekends.*
*Lessons **start** at 9 o'clock every morning.*

Practice

A Put the verbs in brackets ( ) into the correct forms of the Present Simple. For negative verbs, use the short forms (*don't, doesn't*). Sometimes you do not need to change the verb in brackets.

0 Tom catches (catch) the bus to school at about 9 o'clock.
1 It often ________ (rain) at this time of the year.
2 I ________ (not/drive) to work. I go by bus.
3 She usually ________ (have) lunch at about 1 o'clock.
4 He ________ (not/earn) much money in his job.
5 This problem ________ (not/happen) very often.
6 My father ________ (fly) to the USA regularly.
7 Trains to Oxford ________ (leave) every hour in the morning.
8 You ________ (not/do) your work carefully enough.
9 She ________ (read) a newspaper every day.
10 We ________ (not/listen) to the radio very often.
11 He often ________ (arrive) at work late.
12 They ________ (go) to a lot of concerts.

B Complete the questions in the Present Simple.

0 A: Does Alan use ______ a computer?
B: Yes, Alan uses a computer.

1 A: ______ in an office?
B: No, Carol works in a factory.

2 A: Where ______ your games?
B: We play our games in the local park.

3 A: ______ the bus to school?
B: Yes, I take the bus to school every morning.

4 A: When ______?
B: The shops close at 5 o'clock in the afternoon.

5 A: ______ abroad on holiday every year?
B: Yes, we go abroad every year.

6 A: ______ a lot of coffee every day?
B: Yes, I drink about ten cups of coffee every day.

7 A: What kind of car ______?
B: He drives an old German car.

8 A: When ______?
B: The lessons finish at 4.30 every day.

C Complete the dialogues using the Present Simple. For negative verbs, use short forms (*doesn't, don't*).

0 A: Do you watch TV every evening?
B: No, we don't watch ______ TV every evening.

1 A: Does Anna take the bus to work?
B: Yes, she ______ the bus to work at 7 o'clock every morning.

2 A: What time do you have dinner in the evening?
B: We usually ______ dinner at about 8 o'clock in the evening.

3 A: Do you often eat in restaurants?
B: Yes, we often ______ in restaurants.

4 A: Where does Alison teach?
B: She ______ at the university.

5 A: ______ here very often?
B: No, I don't come here very often.

6 A: When ______ in the morning?
B: The post arrives at 8 o'clock in the morning.

7 A: Do you play any sports?
B: No, I ______ any sports. I don't like sport.

8 A: ______ to the office at weekends?
B: No, she doesn't go to work at weekends.

9 A: Where ______ your car every evening?
B: I park my car in the street outside my apartment.

2 Present Continuous (**I'm working**)

1 We form the Present Continuous in this way:

POSITIVE

I	**am/'m**	**working** now.
You / We / They	**are/'re**	
He / She / It	**is/'s**	

NEGATIVE

I	**am not/'m not**	**working** now.
You / We / They	**are not** / **'re not/aren't**	
He / She / It	**is not** / **'s not/isn't**	

QUESTIONS

Where	**am**	I	**working** now?
Where	**are**	you / we / they	
	Is	he / she / it	

2 To make the **-ing** form, we add **-ing**:

walk → walking **go → going**

There are some exceptions:

- verbs ending with **-e**:

  -e → -ing: come → coming

  but: **see → seeing**
- verbs ending with **-ie**:

  -ie → ying: lie → lying
- verbs ending with one vowel (**a,e,i,o,u**) and one consonant (**b,c,d,f,g,k,l,m,n,p** ...):

  -t → -tting: sit → sitting run → running

(For more details, see Table C, on page 95.)

3 Look at this picture of Mike:

We use the Present Continuous for things that are happening now:

*Where's Mike? ~ He's **sitting** outside.*

We also use the Present Continuous for things that are happening for a period of time around now, but not at the moment we speak:

*Mike **is building** his own house.*

Practice

A Complete the sentences about the pictures. Use the correct Present Continuous form of the verb in brackets, and *he/she/they*.

0 

1 

2 

3 

4 

5 

0 He's drinking _____ (drink) a cup of coffee.
1 __________ (carry) their suitcases.
2 __________ (take) a photograph.
3 __________ (sit) on a bench.
4 __________ (run) in a race.
5 __________ (write) a letter.

B Complete the dialogues using the Present Continuous forms of the verbs in brackets ( ), and *I/you/he/she* etc.

0 A: What are you watching ________ (watch) on the TV?
B: I'm watching a programme about wildlife in Africa.

1 A: What ________________ (do) at the moment?
B: He's reading a book.

2 A: ________________ (listen) to me?
B: Yes, of course I'm listening to you.

3 A: Where ________________ (go)?
B: I'm going to the shops.

4 A: What ________________ (cook)?
B: He's cooking an Italian dish.

5 A: Where ________________ (stay)?
B: She's staying with some friends.

6 A: ________________ (wait) for the number 36 bus?
B: No, I'm waiting for a different bus.

7 A: ________________ (rain) at the moment?
B: No, it's quite sunny now.

8 A: What ________________ (read)?
B: I'm reading a very interesting novel.

C Complete the dialogues using the Present Continuous forms of the words in brackets.

0 A: What's Jenny doing?
B: She's talking ________ (She/talk) to her mother on the phone.

1 A: What are John and Michael doing?
B: ________________ (They/play) a game of cards.

2 A: ________________ (the weather/get) better?
B: No, it's very cold outside.

3 A: ________________ (you/leave)?
B: Yes, I have to go home now.

4 A: Where's Harry?
B: ________________ (He/make) a cup of coffee in the kitchen.

5 A: Where's your car?
B: It's at home. ________________ (It/not/work) at the moment.

6 A: ________________ (you/watch) this programme?
B: No, we can watch a different programme if you want.

7 A: Is Michael at home?
B: No, ________________ (he/post) some letters at the post office.

8 A: ________________ (Paul/do) a course?
B: Yes, he's studying Business Management.

3 Present simple (**I go**) or Present Continuous (**I'm going**)

Compare the Present Simple and the Present Continuous:

1

We use the Present Simple to talk about facts (things which are true at any time):
*Anna **speaks** good Spanish.*
*Journalists **write** newspaper articles.*
*I **come** from Norway.* (= I am Norwegian).

We use the Present Continuous to talk about things that are happening now:
*Anna's busy. She**'s speaking** on the phone.*
*What **are** you **writing?** ~ A letter to Jane.*
*Look! The bus **is coming**.*

2

We use the Present Simple for situations that exist for a long time, and for actions that are repeated (e.g. people's habits, or events on a timetable):
*Mike **works** for an advertising company. He **lives** in Paris.* (= His home is in Paris.)

*Jane **travels** a lot in her job.*
*I **do** a lot of sport.*
We can use words like **usually**, **often**, **every**:
*We **usually go** out to dinner at weekends.*
*I **often go** to football matches on Sundays.*
*The buses **leave every hour.***

We use the Present Continuous for things that continue for a limited period of time around now (e.g. holidays, visits, temporary jobs, school or university courses):
*John **is working** in the USA for six weeks. He**'s living** in New York.*

*Jane**'s travelling** around Europe for a month.*
*I**'m doing** a one-year course in tourism.*

3

We use the Present Simple with thinking and feeling verbs (e.g. **know**, **like**, **want**, **love**, **hate**, **remember**):
*I **don't know** which train to catch.*

We do not usually use the Present Continuous with thinking and feeling verbs:
Not ~~*I'm knowing someone who lives in Venice.*~~

Practice

A Complete the sentences with the Present Simple (*I do*) or the Present Continuous (*I am doing*).

0 I leave__________ (leave) home at 7 o'clock every morning.
1 She usually ______________ (work) in the Sales Department in London, but at the moment she ______________ (do) a training course in Bristol.
2 Linda ______________ (wash) her hair every day.
3 He ______________ (try) very hard in every game that he ______________ (play).
4 Excuse me. I think that you ______________ (sit) in my seat.
5 ______________ (you/listen) to the radio very often?
6 Don't talk to me now. I ______________ (write) an important letter.
7 Why ______________ (they/drive) on the left in Britain?

8 It ________________ (not/get) dark at this time of year until about 10 o'clock.

9 It usually ________________ (rain) here a lot, but it ________________ (not/rain) now.

10 A: What are you doing?
B: I ________________ (bake) a cake. Why ________________ (you/smile)? ________________ (I/do) something wrong?

B Two people are standing on a railway station platform. Write the conversation between them, using the Present Simple or the Present Continuous. Sometimes, it is not necessary to change the verb form.

Robert: (Hello. / you / wait / for the same train as me?)
0 Hello. Are you waiting for the same train as me?

Paul: (I / not / know. I / wait / for the 6.15 to Brussels. And you?)
1 ________________

Robert: (Yes, me too. / you / live / in Brussels?)
2 ________________

Paul: (No. I come from Brussels, but I / study / at university in Paris at the moment.)
3 ________________

Robert: (Oh yes? What course / you / take?)
4 ________________

Paul: (I / do / a two-year course in Business Management.)
5 ________________

Robert: (So why / you / go / to Brussels?)
6 ________________

Paul: (All my friends / live / there, and I / often / go / there at weekends.)
7 ________________

(I / not / know / many people in Paris. What about you? / you / often / go / to / Brussels?)
8 ________________

Robert: (Yes, on business. I / go / to a meeting there today.)
9 ________________

Paul: (Oh yes. What kind of job / you / do?)
10 ________________

Robert: (I / work / in the Marketing Department of a small company, and I / often / travel / to different towns and cities for meetings.)
11 ________________

Paul: (What / your company / sell?)
12 ________________

Robert: (It / make / clocks.)
13 ________________

Paul: (Oh look! The train / come.)
14 ________________

4 Past Simple (I walked, she rang)

1 We form the Past Simple of regular verbs by adding **-ed** to the verb:

walk → walked	**watch → watched**
open → opened	**ask → asked**

There are some exceptions:

▶ verbs ending with **-e**:

+ **-d**:	**live → lived**	**like → liked**

▶ verbs ending with a consonant and **-y**:

-y → -ied:	**apply → applied**	**try → tried**

▶ most verbs ending with one vowel and one consonant:

-p → -pped:	**stop → stopped**
	plan → planned

(For more details on the form of the Past Simple, see Table D on page 95.)

2 The Past Simple form of many verbs is irregular:

do → did	**have → had**
take → took	**buy → bought**
come → came	**stand → stood**
find → found	**ring → rang**
go → went	**say → said**

(For more details, see Table E, page 96.)

3 We form the negative with **didn't** and the infinitive (e.g. **do, take, understand**):

*I **didn't understand**.* (Not *~~didn't understood~~*)

We form questions with **did** and the infinitive (e.g. **watch**):

***Did** you **watch** the film?*

4 The Past Simple of **be** is like this:

I/he/she/it **was/wasn't**	} very good.	
You/we/they **were/weren't**		
Was I/he/she/it	} very good?	
Were you/we/they		

5 We use the Past Simple to talk about a completed event in the past. We often say when it happened (e.g. **yesterday, last night**):

*Chris **phoned** me **yesterday**. He **wanted** to discuss something with me.*

***Did** you **enjoy** the concert **last night**?*

6 We can use the Past Simple with **for** to talk about something that continued for a period of time, and ended in the past:

*I **lived** in Rome **for two years**. Then I went to work in Japan.*

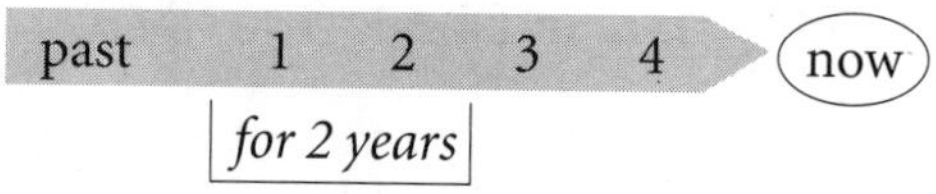

Practice

A Complete the sentences using the Past Simple form and the words in brackets ( ).

0 We _went_ (go) on holiday to Scotland last year.

1 I ________ (take) a taxi from the airport to the city centre.

2 We ________ (walk) to the park and then we ________ (play) tennis.

3 A: ________ (be/your meal) good?

B: No, it ________ (not/be). I ________ (not/like) the vegetables.

4 The man in the shop ________ (say) something to the woman, but she ________ (not/hear) him.

5 I ________ (ring) the doorbell and a woman ________ (open) the door.

6 I ________ (write) a letter to a friend, and then I ________ (post) it.

7 A: ________ (you/understand) the film?

B: No. I ________ (try) to understand it, but the actors ________ (speak) very quickly.

8 He ________ (not/go) to school last Tuesday. He ________ (be) ill.

9 A: ________ (you/buy) some clothes at the market?

B: Yes, I ________ (buy) a pair of trousers and a shirt.

10 A: ________ (you/enjoy) the festival?

B: Yes. It ________ (not/rain) and the music ________ (be) very good.

B Make sentences using the correct form of the Past Simple.

0 (When / you / leave / the party?)

When did you leave the party?

1 (When / you / finish / your exams?)

____

2 (I / wait / for an hour, but he / not / phone.)

____

3 (you / watch / the news on TV last night?)

____

4 (Mark / stop / smoking last month, and he / start / playing tennis again last week.)

____

5 (He / ask / me a question, but I / not / know / the answer.)

____

6 (I / live / there for a few years, but I / not / like / the place.)

____

7 (She / come / to my house yesterday, but she / not / stay.)

____

8 (What / you / say? / I / not / hear / you.)

____

9 (What / you / do / yesterday? / you / go / to school?)

____

C It's the beginning of a new term at college. Two students, Nick and Eric, are talking about the summer holidays. Complete their conversation using the correct Past Simple form of the words in brackets ( ).

Nick: What [0] *did you do* (you/do) in the summer?

Eric: I [1] ________ (take) a trip around Europe by train.

Nick: [2] ________ (it/be) expensive?

Eric: No, I [3] ________ (buy) a railcard, and it [4] ________ (be) quite cheap.

Nick: [5] ________ (you/go) on your own, or with some friends?

Eric: A couple of friends [6] ________ (come) with me.

Nick: How many countries [7] ________ (you/visit)?

Eric: I [8] ________ (go) to six or seven countries. I [9] ________ (have) a great time, and I really [10] ________ (love) all of them.

Nick: Which one [11] ________ (you/like) most?

Eric: Sweden, I think. The countryside [12] ________ (be) marvellous, and I [13] ________ (take) lots of photographs.

Nick: When [14] ________ (you/arrive) back home?

Eric: Last week. I'm still rather tired.

5 Past Continuous (**I was waiting**)

1 We form the Past Continuous in this way:

POSITIVE		
I/he/she/it	**was**	**waiting.**
You/we/they	**were**	
NEGATIVE		
I/he/she/it	**was not/wasn't**	**waiting.**
You/we/they	**were not/weren't**	
QUESTIONS		
Was	I/he/she/it	**waiting?**
Were	you/we/they	

(For rules on the spelling of **-ing** forms (e.g. **waiting**), see Table C on page 95.)

2 Look at this example:

A: *What **were** you **doing** at 7 o'clock last night?*

B: *I **was driving** home from work.*

*I **was living** in Japan in 1991. (I lived there from 1990 to 1993.)*

We use the Past Continuous for an action or situation that was in progress at a particular time in the past (e.g. **at 7 p.m., in 1991**).

3 Now look at this:

*When I **walked** into the room, Ann **was writing** postcards and Keith **was reading**.*

We use the Past Simple (**walked**) for a completed action. We use the Past Continuous (**was writing**) for an action in progress in the past.

4 We can use **when** or **while** before the Past Continuous:

*I met her **when/while** we **were working** for the same company.* (**when** = during the time)

We can only use **when** (not ~~**while**~~) before the Past Simple:

***When I met** her, we were working for the same company.* (**when** = at the time)

Practice

A Complete the sentences by putting the verbs in brackets ( ) into the Past Continuous.

0 It was snowing_________ (snow) when I left home this morning.

1 I tried to explain my problem to her, but she ________________ (not/listen).

2 He ________________ (talk) on the phone when I arrived.

3 A lot of people ________________ (wait) for the 7.30 bus last night.

4 I ________________ (live) in London when I met them.

5 I nearly had an accident this morning. A car ________________ (come) towards me, but I moved quickly out of the way.

6 At the end of the first half of the game, they ________________ (win).

7 It was a sunny afternoon and people ________________ (sit) on the grass in the park. Then it suddenly started to rain.

8 Which hotel ________________ (you/stay) in when you lost your passport?

9 Fortunately, I ________________ (not/drive) too fast when the child walked into the road in front of me.

10 I looked out of the window, and I saw that it ________________ (not/rain) any more.

11 What ________________ (you/do) at 3 o'clock yesterday afternoon?

B **Describe what the people in the picture were doing when Rick came into the room. Use the correct verb from the box in the Past Continuous.**

brush	watch	~~read~~
listen	write	eat
paint	sit	play

0 George _was reading_ a newspaper.

1 Julie ________________ a sandwich.

2 Sue and Liz ________________ table tennis.

3 Frank ________________ television.

4 Caroline ________________ on the floor.

5 Barbara ________________ a letter.

6 Rita ________________ her hair.

7 Alison ________________ to some music.

8 Ann ________________ a picture.

C **Look at this information about Shirley and Kevin and complete the sentences about them, using the Past Continuous (*I was doing*) or the Past Simple (*I did*).**

Shirley		**Kevin**	
1970–76	lived in New York	1972–80	lived in Washington
1973–76	studied at university	1973–75	did a course in Computing
1976	left university	1975–80	worked as a computer operator
1976–80	worked as a translator	1979	met Shirley
1979	met Kevin	1980–85	ran his own company
1982	married Kevin	1982	married Shirley

0 In 1972 Shirley _was living_ in New York.

1 In 1974 Kevin ________________ in Washington.

2 In 1974 Shirley ________________ at university.

3 In 1974 Kevin ________________ a course in Computing.

4 When Shirley ________________ university in 1976, Kevin ________________ as a computer operator.

5 When Kevin ________________ Shirley, she ________________ as a translator.

6 While Shirley ________________ as a translator, she ________________ Kevin.

7 In 1982 Kevin ________________ his own company.

8 While he ________________ his own company, Kevin ________________ Shirley.

6 Present Perfect (I've finished); for, since

1 We form the Present Perfect with **have** or **has** and a past participle (e.g. **finished**):

POSITIVE		
I/you/we/they	**have/'ve**	**finished.**
He/she/it	**has/'s**	
NEGATIVE		
I/you/we/they	**haven't**	**finished.**
He/she/it	**hasn't**	
QUESTIONS		
Have	I/you/we/they	**finished?**
Has	he/she/it	

2 The past participle of regular verbs is the same as the Past Simple form:

+ -ed:	**wash → washed**	**start → started**
+ -d:	**live → lived**	
-y → -ied:	**reply → replied**	
	study → studied	
-p → -pped:	**stop → stopped**	

(For more details, see Table D on page 95.)

For the past participles of irregular verbs, see Table E on page 96.

3 We use the Present Perfect to talk about something that happened in the past, but we do not say exactly when it happened:
*I've **seen** this film **before**.* (**before** = before now)

We often use the Present Perfect in this way for things that happened in the past, and that have a result now:
*I've **seen** this film before. I don't want to see it again now.*
*She's **left** the company. She doesn't work there now.*

We often use the Present Perfect with **ever** (= at any time) and **never** (= at no time):
*Have you **ever** met a famous person?*
*He has **never** worked in a factory.*

4 We can use the Present Perfect with **for** and **since**, to talk about situations or actions in a period of time from the past until now. We use **for** with a period of time (e.g. **three months**), and **since** with a time (e.g. **Tuesday**):
*We've lived here **for six months**.*

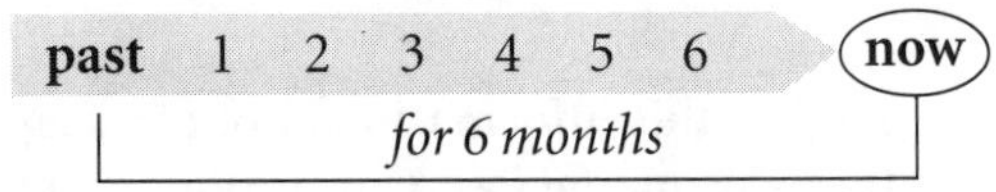

*I haven't seen Tom **since Tuesday**.*

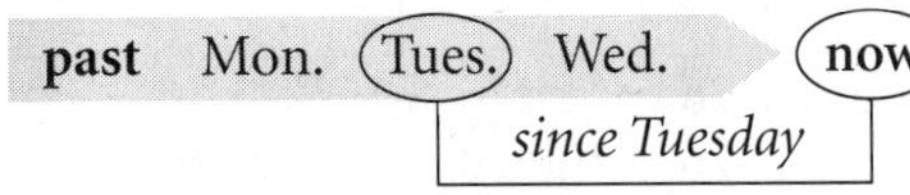

Practice

A **Look at the pictures that show what Jenny has done in her life. Complete the sentences about her, using the Present Perfect form of the verbs in brackets ( ).**

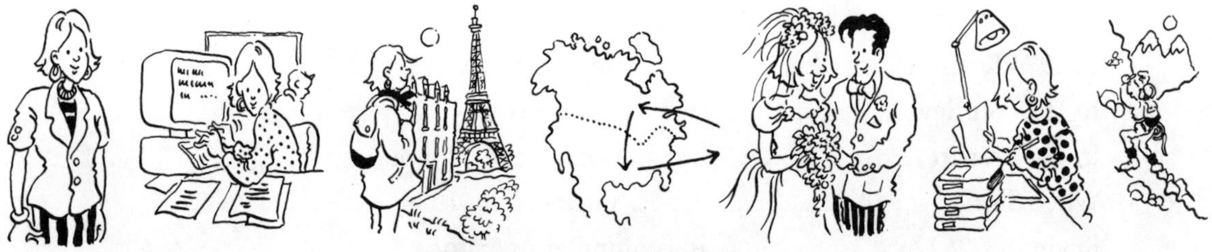

0 She has worked (work) as a secretary and as a schoolteacher.
1 She ____________ (live) in Paris since 1991.
2 She ____________ (visit) Canada and the USA.
3 She ____________ (be) married for 4 years.
4 She ____________ (write) four books.
5 She ____________ (climb) Mont Blanc twice.

B **Complete the sentences using the Present Perfect form of the verbs in brackets ( ).**

0 Don't take my plate away. I haven't finished __________ (not/finish) my meal.

1 A: What's that book about?

B: I don't know. I __________ (not/read) it.

2 I __________ (lose) my pen. Can I borrow yours, please?

3 My father __________ (buy) an expensive, new car.

4 A: I __________ (book) a room here for tonight.

B: Yes madam, what's your name, please?

5 I __________ (make) some sandwiches. Would you like one?

6 I'm not sure what the problem with the car is.

It __________ (not/happen) before.

7 A: __________ (you/reply) to that letter from the bank?

B: No I haven't, but I'll do it soon.

C **Write this conversation using the Present Perfect and the words in brackets ( ).**

Rob: (you / ever / want / to work in another country?)

0 Have you ever wanted to work in another country?

Brian: (Yes, in fact I / work / abroad.)

1 __________

(I / work / in Ireland and in Brazil.)

2 __________

(What about you? / you / ever / have / a job abroad?)

3 __________

Rob: (No, I / never / want / to leave my home town.)

4 __________

(I / live / here for twenty years, and I / never / think / of working abroad.)

5 __________

Brian: (Really? Well, I / apply / for another job abroad.)

6 __________

D **Make sentences with the Present Perfect and *for* or *since*.**

0 (I / not / play / tennis / last summer.)

I haven't played tennis since last summer.

1 (I / know / her / more than ten years.)

____

2 (I / not / eat / anything / lunchtime.)

____

3 (you / live / in this town / a long time?)

____

4 (Jill / be / a good friend / we were at school together.)

____

5 (you / see / Jack / the party last week?)

____

7 Present Perfect with **just, already, yet**

1 We use **just** with the Present Perfect to talk about things that happened a short time before now:

have + **just** + PAST PARTICIPLE		
It has	***just***	*finished.*

*Could I speak to Jane, please? ~ I'm afraid she **has just left**.*
(= She left a short time ago.)
*Is that a good book? ~ I don't know. **I've just started** it.*
(= I started it a short time before now.)

2 Look at this example with **already**:
*Do you want something to eat? ~ No thanks, **I've already eaten.*** (= I ate before now.)
We use **already** with the Present Perfect to emphasize that something happened before now, or before it was expected to happen.
We use **already** like this:

have + **already** + PAST PARTICIPLE			
I've	***already***	*heard*	*that story.*

Here is another example:
Nicola: *Is Sarah going to phone you later?*
Robert: *No. She's* (= She has) *already phoned me.*
(= Sarah phoned before Nicola expected her to phone.)

3 We use **yet** with a negative verb to say that something has not happened, but we think that it will happen:

*The post **hasn't arrived yet.*** (= The post has not arrived, but it probably will arrive.)
*I **haven't finished** this work **yet.*** (= I haven't finished this work, but I will finish it.)
*They **haven't replied** to my letter **yet.***

We use **yet** in questions to ask whether something, that we expect to happen, has happened:
Have you paid** the bill **yet? (= Perhaps you have not paid the bill, but you are going to pay it soon.)
Has it stopped** raining **yet? (= Perhaps it has not stopped raining, but it will stop raining soon.)
Have you found** a job **yet?

Notice that we usually put **yet** at the end of a negative statement or question:
*They haven't replied to my letter **yet**.*
*Have you found a job **yet**?*

Practice

A Complete the dialogues, using *just* and the words in brackets ( ). Use the Present Perfect.

0 A: What's happening in this programme?
B: I don't know. It's just started (It/start).

1 A: ________ (I/come) back from my holiday.
B: Did you have a good time?

2 A: Could I have a copy of *Sports World*, please?
B: Sorry. ________ (I/sell) the last copy.

3 A: How's Lucy?
B: She's very happy. ________ (She/finish) her exams.

4 A: ________ (I/have) a letter from Mike.
B: Oh yes? What did he say?

5 A: Have you heard from Alison and Frank recently?
B: Yes, ________ (they/move) to another town.

6 A: Have you still got the same car?
B: No, ______________________ (I/buy) a new one.

7 A: Would you like something to eat?
B: No, thanks. ______________________ (I/have) breakfast.

B Make sentences using the Present Perfect with *already* or *yet*.

0 (I / not / read / today's newspaper.) yet
I haven't read today's newspaper yet.

1 (you / decide / which one to buy?) yet
____

2 (I / explain / this to you three times.) already
____

3 (Their baby son / start / talking.) already
____

4 (you / phone / Jane?) yet
____

5 (The game / not / finish) yet
____

6 (I / have / lunch) already
____

7 (He / spend / all his money) already
____

C Complete the conversation using *just*, *already* or *yet* and the words in brackets ( ). Put the verbs into the Present Perfect.

Julia: Are you having a good time here?
Anna: Yes, I haven't been here long, and [0] I've already visited (I / visit) a lot of interesting places.
Julia: [1] ______________________ (you / visit / the Art Gallery /?)
Anna: No, [2] ______________________ (I / not / do / that), but I'm going to do it.
Julia: What about the theatre? [3] ______________________ (you / see / a play /?)
Anna: No, but [4] ______________________ (I / book / a ticket) for one. It's called *The Friends*. I rang the theatre five minutes ago. Would you like to come with me?
Julia: Thanks, but [5] ______________________ (I / see / that play). I saw it last month.
Anna: [6] ______________________ (I / read) in the newspaper that *The Adventurers* are giving a concert next week. Do you think it will be good?
Julia: Yes. [7] ______________________ (they / make) a really good, new record. It came out a couple of days ago.
Anna: Will I be able to get a ticket?
Julia: Yes. [8] ______________________ (they / not / sell / all the tickets). But be quick! They're a very popular group.

8 Past Simple (**I lived**) or Present Perfect (**I have lived**)

Compare the Past Simple and the Present Perfect:

1 We use the Past Simple to talk about something that happened at a particular time in the past:

*I **met** John **at 4 o'clock**.*
*When **did** Jane **go** to India? ~ **In June**.*
*Martin **bought** a new car **last week**.*

We use the Present Perfect to talk about the past, but not about when things happened:

***I've met** John's girlfriend. She's nice.*
***Have** you ever **been** to India? ~ Yes, I have.*
*I **have** never **bought** a new car.*

2 We use the Past Simple for situations or actions during a period of time that ENDED in the past:

*I **worked** there **for two years**. I left last year.*

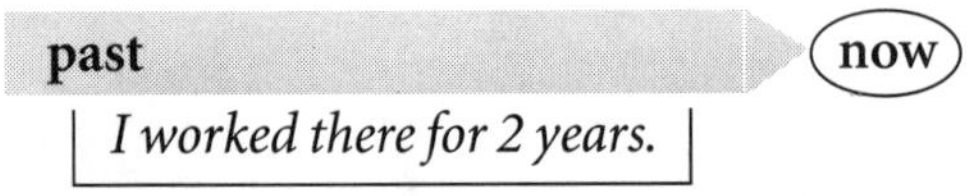

*We **lived** in that house **for a long time**; then we moved to this one.*

*Our company **opened** two new shops **last summer**.*

We use the Present Perfect for situations or actions during a period of time from the past to NOW:

*He **has worked** here **for two years.***
(He still works here.).

*We**'ve lived** in this flat **since we got married**.*
(We still live in it.)

We opened two shops last summer.
***Since then**, we **have opened** two more.*
(**Since then** = since that time)

3 Notice how we often move from the Present Perfect to the Past Simple:

Peter: ***Have** you ever **played** this game before?*
Maria: *Yes, I **played** it once when I was in England.*
Peter: ***Did** you win?*
Maria: *No, I **lost**.*

Practice

A Complete the conversation by choosing the correct form in brackets ( ).

Sarah: 0 Have you ever been (Have you ever been / Did you ever go) to the United States?
Jim: Yes, 1 ________ (I've been / I went) to California last year.
Sarah 2 ________ (Have you liked / Did you like) it?
Jim: Yes, 3 ________ (I've enjoyed / I enjoyed) the trip a lot.
Sarah: What 4 ________ (have you done / did you do) there?
Jim: 5 ________ (I've visited / I visited) Hollywood, Disneyland and San Francisco.
6 ________ (Have you been / Did you go) to California, Sarah?
Sarah: No, but 7 ________ (I've booked / I booked) a holiday there.
I've got my ticket and I'm going next week!

B Complete the dialogues using the Present Perfect (*I have seen*) or Past Simple (*I saw*).

A: I [0] saw ________ (see) Jack last night.
B: Oh really. I [1] ________ (not / see) him for months. How is he?

A: We [2] ________ (go) to the theatre last Saturday.
B: [3] ________ (you / enjoy) the play?
A: Yes, it [4] ________ (be) very good.

A: I [5] ________ (never / hear) of this group before. Are they famous in your country?
B: Yes, they are very popular. They [6] ________ (be) famous in my country for years.

A: What [7] ________ (you / do) last weekend?
B: I [8] ________ (stay) at home. I [9] ________ (need) a rest.

A: [10] ________ (you / ever / win) a competition?
B: Yes, I [11] ________ (win) a photographic competition in 1992.

A: So, John is your best friend. [12] ________ (you / meet) him when you were at university?
B: Yes. We [13] ________ (be) friends for more than ten years.

C Complete this paragraph about the London Underground by putting in the Present Perfect or Past Simple forms of the verbs in brackets ( ).

The London Underground

London [0] has had ________ (have) an underground train system since the 19th Century. The London Underground [1] ________ (start) in 1863, when Victorian engineers and workers [2] ________ (build) the Metropolitan railway. This railway line [3] ________ (go) from Paddington Station to Farringdon Street Station, and steam engines [4] ________ (pull) the coaches. Eight more lines [5] ________ (open) since then. The world's first underground electric railway [6] ________ (open) in 1890. This line [7] ________ (go) from the City of London to Stockwell in South London. The most modern line is the Jubilee line, which [8] ________ (open) in 1977. Since the London Underground [9] ________ (begin), many other cities, such as New York and Moscow, [10] ________ (build) their own systems.

9 Present Perfect Continuous (**I've been cooking**)

1 We form the Present Perfect Continuous in this way:

POSITIVE		
I/you/we/they	**have/'ve**	**been cooking.**
He/she/it	**has/'s**	
NEGATIVE		
I/you/we/they	**haven't**	**been cooking.**
He/she/it	**hasn't**	
QUESTIONS		
Have	I/you/we/they	**been cooking?**
Has	he/she/it	

(For details about **-ing** forms see Table C, on page 95.)

2 We use the Present Perfect Continuous for an action or situation that began in the past and continues until now:

*You're late! **I've been waiting** for you.*

We often use **for** and **since** with the Present Perfect Continuous. We use **for** with a period of time, and **since** with a point in time:

*I've been waiting for you **for two hours.***
*I've been waiting for you **since 6 o'clock.***

3 Here are some more examples:

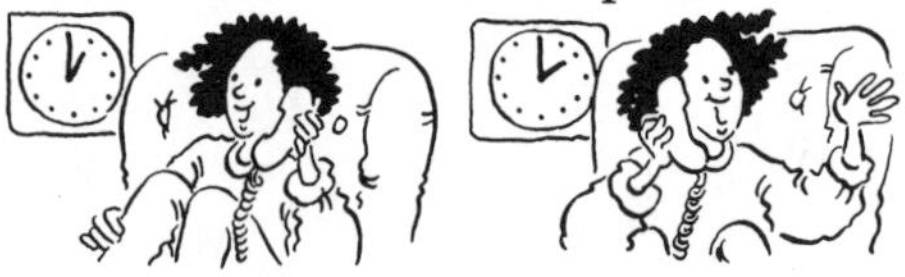

PAST NOW

*Julia **has been talking** on the phone for an hour.* (= She started talking on the phone an hour ago and she is still talking.)

*You**'ve been sitting** there since 1 o'clock.* (= You started sitting there at one o'clock and you are still sitting there.)

4 We use the Present Perfect Continuous for actions that are done many times in a period of time from the past until now:

*She**'s been having** driving lessons for a couple of months.* (= She started a couple of months ago; she is still having lessons.)
***I've been playing** tennis since I was a small child.*

5 We can use **How long** with the Present Perfect Continuous:

*How long **have** you **been living** here?*

Practice

A **Write a sentence for each of the following situations, using the Present Perfect Continuous and *for* or *since*.**

0 She started her course a month ago and she is still doing it.
She has been doing her course for a month.

0 I started reading this novel last weekend and I'm still reading it.
I have been reading this novel since last weekend.

1 It started raining at 3 o'clock and it is still raining.
____

2 He started playing chess when he was 10 and he still plays it.
____

3 I started work at 8 o'clock and I'm still working.
____

4 Helen started looking for another job two months ago and she's still looking.
____

5 We arrived here two hours ago and we're still waiting.
____

B Put *for* or *since* into the gaps.

0 I've been working in this office _since_____ last summer.

1 Have you been doing this course __________ a long time?

2 I've been driving this car __________ more than ten years.

3 She has been planning the party __________ the beginning of the month.

4 George has been telling the same stories __________ several years.

5 We've been waiting for a reply __________ we wrote to them last week.

6 What have you been doing __________ the last time that I saw you?

7 You've been writing that letter __________ more than two hours.

8 He's been feeling ill __________ a few days.

C Complete these dialogues by putting the verbs in brackets ( ) into the Present Perfect Continuous.

A: When did you arrive in London?

B: Two weeks ago.

A: Where 0 _have you been staying_________ (you/stay)?

B: I 1 ______________________________ (stay) with some friends in their flat.

But I am going to move to my own flat next week.

A: Hallo. What are you doing here?

B: I'm waiting to see the manager. I 2 ______________________________

(wait) for half an hour.

A: She's very busy. She 3 ______________________________ (talk) on the

phone to someone all afternoon.

A: I didn't know that you could play the piano.

B: Oh yes, I 4 ______________________________ (have) piano lessons for a year.

A: How long 5 ______________________________ (you/look) for a job?

B: I started looking immediately after I lost my old job. I

6 ______________________________ (apply) for jobs for about six months.

D Choose the best verb from the box to complete each sentence. Use the Present Perfect Continuous form of the verb.

rain	save	study	read
make	~~learn~~	watch	play

0 She _has been learning_____________ Spanish for six months.

1 It ______________________________ for hours; the roads are very wet.

2 We ______________________________ this game for hours. Let's stop!

3 Wendy ______________________________ French at school for three years.

4 I ______________________________ this book for months, but I haven't finished it yet.

5 We ______________________________ this programme for hours.

6 The people next door ______________________________ a lot of noise all day.

7 I ______________________________ my money for a holiday.

10 Past Perfect (**I had finished**)

1 We form the Past Perfect with **had** and a past participle (e.g. **finished**, **gone**):

POSITIVE		
I/you/he/she/it/we/they	**had**	**gone.**
NEGATIVE		
I/you/he/she/it/we/they	**hadn't**	**gone.**
QUESTIONS		
Had	I/you/he/she/it/we/they	**gone?**

(For details on past participle forms, see Table D on page 95, and Table E on page 96.)

2 Look at this example:
*Jane **had gone** home when I phoned her at the office.* (= First, Jane went home. Later, I phoned her.)

3 We use the Past Perfect (e.g. **had gone**) for something that happened before something else in the past. We use the Past Perfect for the thing that happened first; we use the Past Simple (e.g. **phoned**) for the thing that happened later.

Here are some more examples:
*When I got home, I saw that the letter **had arrived**.* (= First, the letter arrived. Later, I got home and I saw it.)

*When he **had finished** his homework, he went to bed.* (= First, he finished his homework. Later, he went to bed.)

*He couldn't pay the bill because he **had left** his wallet at home.* (= First, he left his wallet at home. Later, he couldn't pay the bill.)

*I was very nervous because I **hadn't driven** a car on the motorway **before**.* (**before** = before then)

Note also this example with **by the time** (= when): ***By the time** he was twenty-five, he **had made** a million pounds.*

Practice

A Complete the sentences using the Past Perfect forms of the verbs in brackets ( ).

0 I didn't watch the film because I _had seen_ (see) it before.
1 We couldn't eat at the restaurant because we ________ (not/book) a table.
2 I couldn't buy it because I ________ (spend) all my money.
3 I was tired because I ________ (get up) very early that morning.
4 He didn't know the answer because he ________ (not / do) his homework.
5 She was very happy because she ________ (win) a prize.
6 I ________ (forget) my pen so I had to borrow one.
7 When I got home, I switched on the answerphone. Several people ________ (leave) messages for me.
8 I ________ (not/hear) the joke before; I laughed a lot.
9 When we came out of the restaurant, we saw that our car ________ (disappear).
10 She couldn't see the photographs very well because she ________ (not/bring) her glasses.
11 The ground was very dry; it ________ (not/rain) for a long time.

B **Henry invited some friends to his flat for a meal. Look at the things that he did and didn't do, before his guests arrived. Complete the phrases, using the Past Perfect.**

0 He bought the food.
1 He cleaned the flat.
2 He didn't buy anything to drink.
3 He had a shower.
4 He changed his clothes.
5 He started preparing the meal.
6 He didn't finish preparing the meal.

By the time his guests arrived:

0 *he had bought the food.* __________

1 __________

2 __________

3 __________

4 __________

5 __________

6 __________

C **Complete the sentences so that they mean the same as the pairs of sentences above them. Use the Past Perfect and the Past Simple.**

0 We finished our meal. Then we went for a walk.
When *we had finished our meal, we went for a walk.*

1 I did the course. Then I was able to speak the language well.
When I __________

2 He did all his work. Then he went home.
When __________

3 Everyone left. Then I went to bed.
When __________

4 She had a glass of water. Then she felt better.
When __________

5 He did the washing-up. Then he listened to some music.
When __________

6 Steve saved enough money. Then he bought a new motorbike.
When __________

7 I discussed the problem with a friend. Then I felt happier.
I felt happier when __________

8 She finished speaking. Then I gave my opinion.
I __________ when she __________

9 The guests left. Then we tidied the house.
We __________ when __________

11 Will or be going to

Compare **will** and **be going to**:

1

We use **will** with an infinitive (**do, go, be, arrive** etc.):

	INFINITIVE	
*John **will***	***arrive***	*tomorrow.*

I/you/he (etc.) **will/'ll** **go.**
I/you/he (etc.) **will not/won't** **go.**
Will I/you/he (etc.) **go?**

We use **be going** with **to** + infinitive (**to do, to be, to rain** etc.):

	to + INFINITIVE	
*It's **going***	***to rain***	*soon.*

*My friends **are going to come** tonight.*
*It **isn't going to rain** today.*
*What **are** you **going to do** on Sunday?*

2

We use **will** for actions that we decide to do NOW, at the moment of speaking:

past → now (decision, speaking)

*I like this coat. I think **I'll buy** it.*
A: *What would you like to eat?*
B: ***I'll have** a pizza, please.*

We can use **will** for offers and promises:
***I'll carry** your case for you.* (offer)
*I **won't forget** your birthday again.* (promise)

We use **be going to** for actions that we have decided to do BEFORE we speak:

past (decision) → now (speaking)

***I'm going to clean** my room this afternoon.*
(I decided to clean it this morning.)

We can ask questions about people's plans:
*Which train **are** you **going to catch**?*
(= Which train have you decided to catch?)

3

We use **will** to talk about things that we think or believe will happen in the future:
*I'm sure you**'ll enjoy** the film.*
*I'm sure it **won't rain** tomorrow. It**'ll be** another beautiful, sunny day.*

We use **be going to** for something that we expect to happen, because the situation now indicates that it is going to happen:
*He's running towards the goal, and he**'s going to score**.*

Practice

A **Look at the pictures and complete the sentences about what we can see is going to happen. Use *be going to* and the words in the box.**

take	catch
~~eat~~	land
jump	knock

0 He's going to eat his meal.
1 The plane ______________________.
2 She ______________________ a picture.
3 He ______________________ into the water.
4 She ______________________ on the door.
5 He ______________________ the ball.

B Make sentences with *'ll* and the words in brackets ( ).

0 Sit down. (I / make / you a cup of coffee.) I'll make you a cup of coffee.

1 A: It's time for me to go home.
B: (I / give / you a lift.) ______

2 (I / phone / you tonight, I promise.) ______

3 A: I won't be able to buy the tickets for the concert today.
B: Don't worry. (I / buy / the tickets for both of us, and I / meet / you at the concert hall.) ______

4 A: Oh no, it's raining and I must go to the shops.
B: That's okay. (I / lend / you my umbrella.) ______

C Complete these sentences using the correct form of *am/is/are going to* and the words in brackets ( ).

0 I keep sneezing. I'm going to get (get) a bad cold.

1 Some of my friends ______ (have) a party next week. They've invited lots of people.

2 I ______ (play) tennis this afternoon. I've booked a court.

3 We ______ (move) to a different area of the town because we don't like this area.

4 Anna ______ (look) for a different job. She wants to do something more interesting.

5 They said on the radio that it ______ (rain) this afternoon.

D Complete the sentences, using the words in brackets and *'ll* or a form of *be going to.*

0 A: It's rather hot in here, isn't it?
B: Yes, you're right. I'll open (I/open) a window.

1 A: Are you going to watch TV tonight?
B: Yes, ______ (I/watch) my favourite programme at 9 o'clock.

2 A: What ______ (you/eat) tonight? What food have you bought?
B: I haven't bought any food.
A: Well, why don't you come to my house? ______ (I/cook) us something nice to eat.

3 A: I'm going into the centre of town tomorrow. ______ (I/buy) some new clothes.
B: Oh, what ______ (you/get)?
A: ______ (I/look) for a T-shirt and some jeans.
B: I'd like to go into the centre too. ______ (I/come) with you.

4 A: ______ (I/leave) work late tomorrow. There is a meeting at 6 p.m.
B: Oh, I didn't know that. Well, ______ (I/see) you after the meeting.

5 ______ (I/phone) Tom at 6 o'clock. I promised to phone him this evening.

6 A: Are you going to have a holiday in the summer?
B: Yes, ______ (I/travel) around Europe with a friend.

12 Present Continuous for the future (**I'm leaving tomorrow**)

1 We can use the Present Continuous (see unit 2) to talk about the future:

A: *Where **are** you **going** next week?*
B: *We**'re flying** to Switzerland. We**'re staying** in the Alps for a week.*

2 We use the Present Continuous to talk about future arrangements. Arrangements are plans of action that we have agreed with other people:

*I**'m meeting** some friends at a disco tonight.*
(= I have talked to my friends, and we have agreed a time and place to meet.)

*Mary **is starting** a course on Monday.*
(= She has registered at a school for a particular course.)

*He**'s getting** a new car on Monday.*
(= He has chosen the car and has arranged to buy it.)

*I**'m not doing** anything this weekend.*
(= I have no particular plans; I haven't arranged to do anything.)

3 When we talk about future plans, we can often use either the Present Continuous or **be going to**, but compare:

PRESENT CONTINUOUS: *We**'re moving** to a new flat in two weeks.* (= We have found the flat, signed the contract, and agreed a date to move.)
be going to: *We**'re going to move** to a new flat soon.* (= We intend to move but we don't know when; we have not found a flat.)

We use the Present Continuous for a definite arrangement. We use **be going to** for something that we intend to do, but that we may not have arranged. Here is another example:

> *I**'m meeting** Diana at 3 p.m., and **I'm going to meet** her assistant some time next week.* (= I have arranged to meet Diana, and I intend to meet her assistant.)

Practice

A **These are the arrangements for a trip that you and a friend are taking next week.**

4-Day trip to Madrid	
Tuesday:	flight leaves at 18.00; check in at the *Hotel Princess*
Wednesday:	visit the Prado Museum, morning; take a guided tour of the Royal Palace, afternoon
Thursday:	have a special lunch at the hotel; see an opera at the Opera House, evening
Friday:	leave Madrid at 11.00.

Complete these sentences using the Present Continuous form of these verbs:

have ~~go~~ see fly stay leave take visit

0 *We're going* ______ on a 4-day trip to Madrid next week.
1 ______ to Madrid at 18.00 on Tuesday.
2 ______ in the Hotel Princess.
3 ______ the Prado Museum on Wednesday morning.
4 ______ a guided tour of the Royal Palace on Wednesday afternoon.
5 ______ a special lunch at the hotel on Thursday.
6 ______ an opera at the Opera House on Thursday evening.
7 ______ Madrid at 11.00 on Friday.

B Look at this page from Laura's diary for next week and complete the sentences about her plans, using the Present Continuous.

Monday:	work until 6 o'clock; go to the library after work.
Tuesday:	play tennis with Ian, 5 o'clock.
Wednesday:	go to the doctor's, 2.30
Thursday:	have a typing lesson, 10.30–12.30
Friday:	meet Jackie outside cinema, 8.30. Film starts at 9.
Saturday:	Nick & Lucy come here for dinner
Sunday:	______________

0 *She's working* ______ until 6 on Monday.
1 ____________ to the library after work on Monday.
2 ____________ tennis with Ian at 5 on Tuesday.
3 ____________ to the doctor's at 2.30 on Wednesday.
4 ____________ a typing lesson from 10.30 to 12.30 on Thursday.
5 ____________ Jackie outside the cinema at 8.30 on Friday.
6 ____________ a film at 9 on Friday.
7 Nick and Lucy ____________ to her house for dinner on Saturday.
8 ____________ anything on Sunday.

C Look at George's timetable for tomorrow and complete the conversation that follows it, using the Present Continuous and the words in brackets ( ).

9 o'clock:	catch the train
10 o'clock:	meet Judy in the main square
11 o'clock:	meet Harry and Fred for coffee
12 o'clock:	go to the theatre box office for tickets
1 o'clock:	have lunch with Dave
2–5 o'clock:	help Dave in his bike shop
6 o'clock:	catch the train home

Tim: What [0] *are you doing* ______ (you/do) tomorrow, George?
George: [1] ____________ (I/go) into the town centre.
Tim: What time [2] ____________ (you/catch) the train?
George: At 9 o'clock. [3] ____________ (I/meet) Judy at 10.
Tim: Where [4] ____________ (you/meet) her?
George: In the main square, and then [5] ____________ (we/meet) Harry and Fred in a café. After that, [6] ____________ (we/go) to the theatre to buy some tickets, and then [7] ____________ (I/have) lunch with Dave.
Tim: What [8] ____________ (you/do) in the afternoon?
George: [9] ____________ (I/help) Dave in his shop.
Tim: When [10] ____________ (you/come) home?
George: [11] ____________ (I/catch) the train back at 6.

13 Conditionals (**If I am . . .**)

1 Look at this:

If + PRESENT SIMPLE + PRESENT SIMPLE	
*If I **eat** too much,*	*I **feel** bad.*

(= Every time I eat too much, I feel bad.)

We use this structure (**if** + Present Simple, + Present Simple) for facts that are generally true:

*If I **don't get** enough sleep, I **feel** tired.* (= Every time I don't get enough sleep, I feel tired.)

*If you **want** to become a doctor, you **have** to study hard.* (= Anyone who wants to become a doctor has to study hard.)

2 We can say the same thing by reversing the two parts of the sentence:

PRESENT SIMPLE + if + PRESENT SIMPLE	
*I **feel** bad*	*if I **eat** too much.*

Note that we do not use a comma (,) before **if**.

3 Now look at this:

If + PRESENT SIMPLE + will/won't	
*If I'**m** late,*	*she'**ll be** angry.*

(= Perhaps I will be late; then she'll be angry.)

We use this structure (**if** + Present Simple + **will/won't**) to talk about things that may happen in the future. The verb after **if** is Present Simple, but we use it for a possible future action or situation; we use **will/won't** + verb for the result:

future possibility + result	
*If we **don't hurry**,*	*we **won't finish**.*

4 We can reverse the order:

*She'll be angry **if** I'm late.*

*We won't finish **if** we don't hurry.*

5 We do not use **will/won't** after **if**:

Not ~~*If I will be late, she'll be angry.*~~

Practice

A Put these facts about various types of people into sentences with *if* + Present Simple, + Present Simple. Make *you* the subject of both parts of the sentence.

0 Doctors treat people who are ill.
If you're a doctor, you treat people who are ill.

1 Vegetarians don't eat meat.
If you're a vegetarian, ______

2 People who live in a hot country don't like cold weather.
If you live ______

3 Teachers have to work very hard.
If you're a teacher, ______

4 People who do a lot of exercise stay fit and healthy.
If you ______

5 Mechanics understand engines.
If you're a ______

6 People who read newspapers know what's happening in the world.
______

B Complete these sentences with *if* + Present Simple, + *will/won't*, using the words in brackets. Sometimes you do not need to change the words in brackets ( ).

0 If _it rains_ (it/rain), _we won't go_ (we/not/go) out.

1 If ________ (the weather/be) nice tomorrow, ________ (we/drive) to the coast.

2 If ________ (she/post) the letter now, ________ (they/receive) it tomorrow.

3 ________ (the boss/be) angry if ________ (John/arrive) at work late again.

4 ________ (I/go) to their party if ________ (I/have) enough time.

5 If ________ (she/not/pass) this exam, ________ (she/not/get) the job that she wants.

6 ________ (you/learn) a lot if ________ (you/take) this course.

7 If ________ (I/get) a ticket, ________ (I/go) to the concert.

8 ________ (I/buy) that camera if ________ (it/not/cost) too much.

9 If ________ (you/run) very fast, ________ (you/catch) the bus.

10 ________ (I/go) to the doctor's if ________ (I/not/feel) better tomorrow.

11 If ________ (they/win) this game, ________ (they/be) the champions.

C Complete the dialogues with the Present Simple or *will/won't* forms of the words in brackets ( ). Sometimes you do not need to change the words in brackets.

0 A: We must be at the airport at 2 o'clock.
B: Well, if _we take_ (we/take) a taxi at 1 o'clock, _we won't be_ (we/not/be) late.

1 A: I'd like a newspaper.
B: Well, ________ (I/buy) one for you if ________ (I/go) to the shop later.

2 A: Has John phoned yet?
B: No, and if ________ (he/not/phone) this afternoon, ________ (I/phone) him this evening.

3 A: Is Fiona there, please?
B: No, but if ________ (you/want) to leave a message, ________ (I/give) it to her.

4 A: Is Tim going to pass his exam?
B: Well, ________ (he/fail) if ________ (he/not/work) harder.

5 A: Could I have some information about this year's concerts, please?
B: Yes, if ________ (you/fill in) this form, ________ (I/send) it to you in the post.

14 Present tense verbs with **when, before, after, until** etc.

1 Look at this sentence:
__When__ the programme __ends__, I'll do the washing-up.

To talk about an event in the future, we usually use the Present Simple (e.g. **ends**) after **when**, **before**, **after**, **until** and **as soon as**. We do not use **will**:
I'm going to finish this work __before I go__. (Not ~~*. . . before I will go.*~~)
Wait here __until__ I __get__ back.
I'll phone you __as soon as__ I __arrive__.

2 We can use **when** + Present Simple to refer to a time when something will happen:
I'll buy an ice-cream __when I'm__ in the newsagent's.

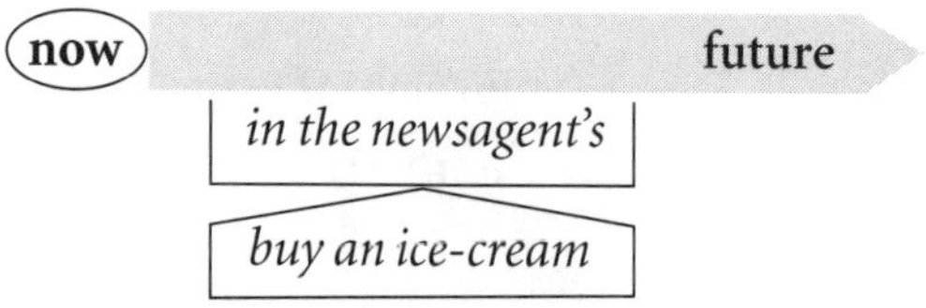

__When__ you __see__ her, give her my message.

We use **until** + Present Simple to mean from now to a time in the future:
We'll sit outside __until__ it __gets__ dark. (= We'll sit outside from now to when it gets dark.)

We use **as soon as** + Present Simple with the meaning 'immediately after':
They'll start playing __as soon as__ it __stops__ raining. (= They will start playing immediately after the rain stops.)

3 We use **when** + Present Perfect (e.g. I **have done**) to talk about an action that must, or will, happen before the next action can happen:
__When I've found__ a job, I'll look for a place to live. (= First I will find a job; then I will look for a place to live.)

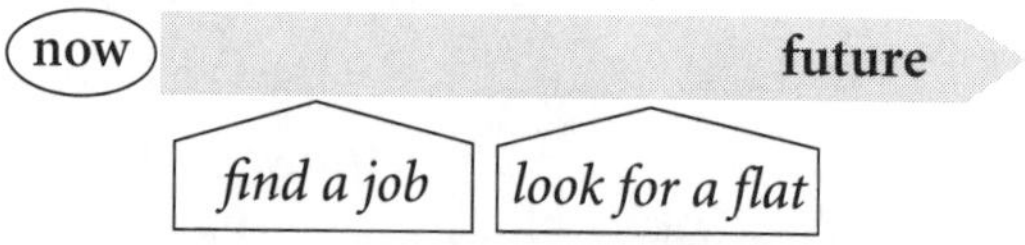

__When__ Simon __has saved__ enough money, he'll buy a car. (= First Simon must save the money; then he can buy a car.)

4 With **after** we can use either the Present Simple or the Present Perfect with no difference in meaning:
After she __takes/has taken__ the course, she'll be a qualified teacher. (= When she has done her course, she'll be a qualified teacher.)

Practice

A Complete the sentences by putting *when, before, after, as soon as* or *until* into the gaps. Sometimes more than one answer is possible.

0 I'll stay in this job until__________ I find a better one.
1 I'm going to keep working ______________ I finish this.
2 Remember to buy some stamps ______________ you're in the post office.
3 ______________ I speak to him on the phone tonight, I'll ask him.
4 We can go for a meal ______________ we've seen the film.
5 I'll keep looking for it ______________ I find it.
6 I'll wait for them ______________ it gets dark, and then I'll leave.
7 Don't forget to lock the door ______________ you go out.
8 ______________ I've found the information, I'll phone you.
9 We'll wait ______________ it stops raining, and then we'll go out.
10 ______________ you see John, give him my regards.
11 Put in your application ______________ the closing date arrives.
12 You shouldn't wait. You should reply ______________ you receive the invitation.
13 Book a table ______________ you go to the restaurant. It's often full.

B Complete the dialogues, using the Present Simple or *will* forms of the verbs in brackets ( ). Sometimes you do not need to change the word in brackets.

0 A: Could you post this letter for me today, please?
B: Yes, I 'll do ____________ (do) it when I go ____________ (go) to the shops.

1 A: I might be late tonight.
B: OK. I ____________ (wait) until you ____________ (arrive).

2 A: I'm leaving next week.
B: I ____________ (see) you before you ____________ (go), won't I?

3 A: Have you decided what you're going to do at the weekend yet?
B: No, but I ____________ (phone) you as soon as I ____________ (know) what I'm going to do.

4 A: Have you done that homework yet?
B: No, not yet. I ____________ (do) it when I ____________ (have) enough time.

5 A: I don't want to go to that party tonight.
B: Well, I'm sure you ____________ (enjoy) it when you ____________ (get) there.

6 A: Could you tell Tom to ring me, please?
B: Yes, I ____________ (tell) him when I ____________ (see) him tomorrow.

7 A: Mr Jackson isn't in at the moment.
B: I see. Well, I ____________ (wait) until he ____________ (come) back.

8 A: Have you booked a hotel in London yet?
B: No, but we ____________ (book) one before we ____________ (go) there.

9 A: Don't forget to write to Peter.
B: OK. I ____________ (do) it as soon as I ____________ (get) home.

10 A: ____________ (you/see) Jack when you ____________ (be) in Madrid?
B: Yes, I hope I will. I ____________ (phone) him when I ____________ (arrive) in Madrid.

C Complete the sentences using the Present Perfect or *will* forms of the verbs in brackets.

0 When you have written ____________ (write) that letter, I'll post ____________ (post) it for you.
1 I ____________ (pay) the bill when I have borrowed some money from somebody.
2 When I've found a car that I want to buy, I ____________ (ask) my bank to lend me the money to buy it.
3 After the plane ____________ (land), you may unfasten your safety belts.
4 When you ____________ (check) all your answers, hand in your question paper.
5 I ____________ (read) this book when I'm on holiday.
6 When I ____________ (read) this magazine, I'll start work.
7 You ____________ (feel) better when you have had something to eat.
8 When you ____________ (finish) your work, you can go home.
9 She ____________ (be) pleased when she hears the news.
10 Let's go for a walk after we ____________ (have) dinner.

15 So am I. I am too. Neither am I. I'm not either.

1 Look at this:

She is saying that she is also tired.

2 Here are some more examples:

*He **was** very angry.* ~ *So **was I**.*

My flat's quite small. ~ *So **is mine**.*
*They **were** waiting.* ~ *So **was she**.*
***I'm** going to have tea.* ~ *So **am I**.*

*Ann **has** finished her work and so **has Mary**.*
*They**'ve** been waiting* ~ *So **has she**.*

*I **work** in an office* ~ *So **do I**.*
*I **enjoyed** the film.* ~ *So **did I**.*

*Philip **will** pass the exam and so **will you**.*
*He **can** drive.* ~ *So **can she**.*

Note:

- ▶ we use **so** after a positive statement;
- ▶ the verb we use after **so** depends on the verb used in the positive statement.

3 Instead of **so am I**, we can say **I am too**, with the same meaning. Here are some examples:

I'm tired. ~ ***I am** too.*
We've got a small flat. ~ ***We have** too.*
I work in an office. ~ ***I do** too.*
*Bill enjoyed the film and **I did** too.*
He can drive. ~ ***She can** too.*

4 We can use expressions like **neither am I** to reply to a negative statement:

I'm not tired. ~ *Neither **am I**.*
(= And I'm not tired.)
I haven't seen that film ~ *Neither **have I**.*
I don't like this place. ~ *Neither **do I**.*
I didn't see that play. ~ *Neither **did I**.*
*His sister can't drive and neither **can he**.*

5 We can say **I'm not either** to mean the same as **neither am I:**

I'm not tired. ~ ***I'm not** either.*
(= And I'm not tired.)
I haven't seen that film. ~ ***I haven't** either.*
I don't like this place. ~ ***I don't** either.*
I didn't see that play. ~ ***I didn't** either.*
*His sister can't drive and **he can't** either.*

Practice

A Complete the sentences with *so, too, either* or *neither*.

0 I really enjoyed that meal. ~ So did I.
0 I haven't done the homework. ~ I haven't either.
0 We live in the centre of town. ~ We do too.
1 I don't like football. ~ __________ do I.
2 I haven't been to America. ~ __________ have I.
3 My father works in an office. ~ __________ does mine.
4 I haven't read a newspaper today. ~ __________ have I.
5 I play a lot of different sports. ~ I do __________.
6 I've been working very hard lately. ~ __________ have I.
7 Ann will be at the party and __________ will Jane.
8 My brother can't speak any foreign languages and __________ can my sister.
9 Helen sent me a birthday card and Robin did __________.
10 George isn't going to the meeting and I'm not __________.
11 Tony arrived late and __________ did I.
12 Kathy didn't go to the concert and __________ did I.

B Put in the replies, using *so* or *neither* and the words in brackets, as in the examples.

QUESTIONS			ANSWERS
0 I've got a cold.	(I)	~	So have I.
0 I haven't got much money.	(I)	~	Neither have I.
1 We're going to the concert.	(we)	~	______
2 My pen doesn't work.	(mine)	~	______
3 I haven't read today's paper.	(I)	~	______
4 My meal was excellent.	(mine)	~	______
5 I've been ill.	(Frank)	~	______
6 Ron didn't go to the party.	(George)	~	______
7 I can't understand this game.	(I)	~	______
8 I'm not working tomorrow.	(I)	~	______
9 Ruth passed the exam.	(John)	~	______
10 I've eaten enough.	(I)	~	______
11 I'm going to see that film.	(we)	~	______
12 My car is very old.	(mine)	~	______

C Look at the information in the table about four people and complete the sentences using *so*, *too*, *either* or *neither*.

	JULIA	ROBERT	SANDRA	PAUL
Lives in:	*New York*	*Chicago*	*New York*	*Los Angeles*
Speaks:	*Spanish*	*French*	*Spanish*	*French*
Drives?	*Yes*	*No*	*No*	*Yes*
Likes:	*reading*	*travelling*	*travelling*	*reading*
Plays:	*basketball*	*basketball*	*tennis*	*tennis*

0 Julia lives in New York and Sandra does too.
0 Julia lives in New York and so does Sandra.
1 Robert doesn't live in New York and ______ Paul.
2 Robert doesn't live in New York and Paul ______.
3 Julia speaks Spanish and ______ Sandra.
4 Julia speaks Spanish and Sandra ______.
5 Robert can't speak Spanish and ______ Paul.
6 Robert can't speak Spanish and Paul ______.
7 Julia can drive and Paul ______.
8 Robert can't drive and ______ Sandra.
9 Julia has passed her driving test and ______ Paul.
10 Robert likes travelling and ______ Sandra.
11 Julia likes reading and Paul ______.
12 Julia plays basketball and ______ Robert.
13 Sandra doesn't play basketball and ______ Paul.

16 Verb + preposition (**wait for, listen to**)

1 After some verbs we use a particular preposition (e.g. **for, to, on**):

VERB + PREPOSITION
wait for: *I was **waiting for** a bus.*
listen to: *She **listens to** the radio a lot.*
belong to: *Does that book **belong to** you?*
ask for: *Have you **asked for** the bill?*
apply for: *He has **applied for** another job.*
depend on: *The salary **depends on** your age.*
agree with: *I don't **agree with** you.*

2 Now look at these examples:

▸ **arrive at / in:**

*We **arrived at** the **airport**.* (You **arrive at** a place, for example a building.)

*We **arrived in Portugal**.* (You **arrive in** a town or country.)

▸ **look at / for:**

***Look at** that strange **man** over there!* (You **look at** something you can see.)

*I'm **looking for** my **diary**.* (You **look for** something that you are trying to find.)

▸ **talk to / about:**

*She was **talking to** some **friends**.* (You **talk to** somebody.)

*They were **talking about politics**.* (You **talk about** something.)

3 In questions that begin with a question word like **What, Who** or **How many**, we usually put the preposition at the end:

***Who** are you waiting **for**?*

***Who** does this jacket belong **to**?*

4 We do not usually use a preposition after these verbs:

phone/ring: *He **phoned/rang** me last night.* (Not ~~*He phoned/rang to me*~~ ...)
discuss: *We often **discuss** sport.* (Not ... ~~*discuss about sport*~~.)
answer: *She didn't **answer** me.* (Not ... ~~*answer to me*~~.)
reach (= arrive): *I **reached** the office at 9 o'clock.* (Not ... ~~*reached to the office*~~ ...)

5 Note that we **pay someone**, but we **pay for something**:

*She paid **him** yesterday.* (You **pay** a person.)

*I paid **for the books**.* (You **pay for** something that you receive.)

But note that we **pay** a bill:

*I'll pay **the bill**.*

Practice

A Complete these sentences with the correct prepositions (*to, for*, etc). In some sentences no preposition is required.

0 I'm waiting <u>for</u> a telephone call.
0 We reached <u>—</u> the airport after 11 o'clock.
1 I'll ask ______ some information.
2 Let's listen ______ some music.
3 Where do I pay ______ this shirt?
4 Let's discuss ______ the arrangements for tomorrow.
5 Who's going to pay ______ the taxi driver?
6 We paid ______ the bill and left the restaurant.
7 I'll phone ______ the theatre and book two tickets.
8 The price of the holiday depends ______ when you want to travel.
9 He walked out of the room without answering ______ me.
10 A lot of people don't agree ______ you.
11 I've applied ______ a visa.
12 Who does this pen belong ______ ?

B Complete the story by putting a preposition into the gaps if one is necessary. For some gaps no preposition is required.

When Jack arrived [0] at the theatre, Alice was waiting [1] ______ him. 'Where have you been?' she asked [2] ______ him. 'We can talk [3] ______ that later,' said Jack. 'I tried to phone [4] ______ you to say that I was going to be late, but you were out. Let's go into the concert.' 'OK,' said Alice, 'but you have to pay [5] ______ the tickets! The man should always pay.' 'I don't agree [6] ______ you,' said Jack, 'but I will pay if I can. It just depends [7] ______ how much they cost. I haven't brought much money with me.'

C Complete the questions. The replies will help you. Be careful to put the verbs in the correct tense.

0 A: Who does this car belong to?
B: It belongs to the man who lives next door.

1 A: What kind of music do you listen ______?
B: I listen to classical music and I also listen to some rock.

2 A: What was he ______?
B: He was talking about his trip to China.

3 A: How many jobs have you ______?
B: I've applied for five jobs.

4 A: Who ______?
B: I'm waiting for Mary. We agreed to meet here at 4 o'clock.

5 A: What ______?
B: I'm looking for my glasses.

6 A: What ______?
B: She asked for some money.

D Complete the postcard by putting in the prepositions that are necessary. Sometimes, no preposition is required.

Dear Sam,

We arrived [0] in Greece at about 11 o'clock. We got a taxi from the airport to the port, and then we took a lovely, little boat to the island. I enjoyed looking [1] ______ the scenery on the way. When we reached [2] ______ the island, we looked [3] ______ our villa but we couldn't find it. I talked [4] ______ a local man, and I asked [5] ______ directions. He offered to take me there. When we arrived [6] ______ the villa, I offered to pay [7] ______ him, but he didn't want any money. The weather's lovely. I'll ring [8] ______ you when we get back from our holiday.

Love,

Tina

17 Make, do, have, get

1 There are many phrases in which a particular verb is used together with a particular noun, for example:
__make__ a cup of __coffee__
__do__ some __work__
__have breakfast__

2 We often use **make** in sentences about producing or creating something:
They __made__ a __fire__ in the woods.
Shall I __make__ some __coffee__?
He __made__ some __sandwiches__ for lunch.

3 We also use **make** in these phrases:
Excuse me. I have to __make__ a __phone call__.
He __makes__ a lot of __mistakes__ in his work.
I couldn't sleep because the neighbours were __making__ a lot of __noise__.

4 We often use **do** in sentences about working, or about doing particular jobs:
Have you __done__ your __homework__?
He offered to __do__ the __washing-up__.
We're going to __do__ some __shopping__.
I haven't __done__ much __work__ today.

5 We use **have** + noun to describe activities:
I'm going to __have__ a __shower__ in the morning.
We usually __have lunch__ at about 1 o'clock.
I'm __having fish__ for dinner tonight.
I __had__ a __swim__ in the sea this morning.

6 We use **get** with adjectives that describe feelings, to say that we begin to have the feeling:
I'm __getting tired__ now. I need a rest.
They're late and I'm __getting worried.__
I __got angry__ and shouted at them.

7 We use **get** in some phrases that describe a change of situation:
We __got lost__ in Paris. (= We became lost ...)
It's __getting cold__. (= It's becoming cold.)
Jane was very ill, but she's __getting better__.
They __got married__ three years ago.
It rained heavily and I __got__ very __wet__.

8 We use **make** + someone + **adjective** to talk about the cause of a feeling:
He __made us__ very __angry__.
The news __made him happy__.

Practice

A Complete the sentences, using the correct forms of *make, do, have* or *get*. Be careful that you use the correct tense.

0 He was __making__ a cup of coffee in the kitchen.
0 We __had__ lunch in a very pleasant little restaurant yesterday.
1 She always ________ excited before her birthday.
2 A: Helen's ill.
B: Oh dear. I hope she will ________ better soon.
3 We have to ________ some homework every evening.
4 I think I've ________ a terrible mistake.
5 They ________ the shopping and then they went home.
6 I was late because I ________ lost on my way there.
7 It always ________ very hot here during the summer.
8 Could I ________ a quick phone call, please?
9 Please don't ________ so much noise.
10 It was a lovely surprise and it ________ me very happy.
11 Her parents are ________ old. They are sixty or seventy.
12 How old were you when you ________ married?

B **Look at the notes in the box about what Laura did yesterday. Complete the sentences, using the correct forms of *make, do, have* or *get.* Sometimes more than one answer is possible.**

7.30	Got up. Shower.
8.00	Breakfast. (fruit juice and toast)
8.30 – 9.00	Walk to work. Rain.
9.00 – 1.00	Work. Very busy.
1.00 – 2.00	Lunch in office. Sandwiches.
2.00 – 5.00	Work. Finished everything.
5.30	Shopping. Home.
7.00	Pizza for dinner. Washed up.
8.00 – 11.00	TV. Tired. Bed.

It was a normal day for Laura yesterday. She got up at 7.30 and she 0 had______ a shower. Then she 1 ______ breakfast. For breakfast she 2 ______ cornflakes and toast. While she was walking to work, it rained and she 3 ______ wet. She 4 ______ angry about this. In the morning she 5 ______ a lot of work. She 6 ______ lunch at about 1 o'clock. She 7 ______ sandwiches for lunch. When she had 8 ______ all her work in the afternoon, she went home. On the way home she 9 ______ some shopping.

She 10 ______ a pizza for dinner. She 11 ______ the washing-up and then she watched TV for three hours. By eleven o'clock she felt quite tired, and so she went to bed.

C **Complete the dialogues, using the correct form of *make, do, have* or *get.***

0 A: Was the film good?
B: No, I got______ bored in the middle of it.

1 A: Could you ______ some shopping for me?
B: Yes, what do you want me to buy?

2 A: Were you pleased by the news?
B: No, it ______ me very unhappy.

3 A: Was it a warm day?
B: Yes, but it ______ rather cold in the evening.

4 A: Are you hungry at the moment?
B: No, I ______ a big meal a couple of hours ago.

5 A: Did he pass the test?
B: No, he ______ a lot of mistakes.

6 A: Are you ready to go out?
B: No, I'm not. I want to ______ a wash first.

7 A: Could you repair this for me?
B: Yes, but I can't ______ the job until tomorrow.

18 Word order: subject, verb, object etc.

1 Look at this table:

SUBJECT	+ VERB	+ OBJECT
Our firm	*makes*	*computers.*
I	*posted*	*the letter.*
She	*caught*	*the train.*
The phone	*doesn't work.*	
He	*was eating*	*a sandwich.*

Sentences must have a subject and a verb. If there is an object, it usually goes after the verb. Any other information, such as a time, a place etc, usually follows the object:

SUBJECT	+ VERB	+ OBJECT	+ PLACE
She	*met*	*Tom*	*in Rome.*

(Not ~~*She met in Rome Tom.*~~)

2 We put an adjective before a noun:

	ARTICLE	+ ADJECTIVE	+ NOUN
She has	*a*	*blue*	*dress.*

We put an adjective after **be**, **get**, and **seem**:

	VERB	+ ADJECTIVE
She	***is***	*clever.*
He	***seems***	*nice.*

3 We usually put a place before a time:

	+ PLACE	+ TIME
He worked	*in a factory*	*for a year.*
They've been	*here*	*since 2.*
We met	*in France*	*last June.*
I walked	*around the town*	*yesterday.*

4 We usually put a direction before a time:

	+ DIRECTION	+ TIME
The bus arrived	*from Liverpool*	*at 10.30.*
He came	*to this country*	*in 1985.*
They moved	*into the flat*	*yesterday.*

5 Look at the word order in these questions:

	VERB	+ SUBJECT	+ VERB	+ OBJECT
When	*did*	*you*	*join*	*the club?*
				+ PLACE
	Can	*you*	*come*	*here?*
				+ DIRECTION
When	*are*	*you*	*going*	*to the USA?*
				+ TIME
What	*are*	*you*	*doing*	*tonight?*

Practice

A **Put the words in brackets ( ) into the correct order to make a sentence.**

0 (me – she – at half past 4 – phoned)

She phoned me at half past 4.

1 (my coat – where – you – put – did – ?)

____

2 (from the airport – took – we – a taxi)

____

3 (three weeks ago – the job – started – she)

____

4 (around Europe – last summer – travelled – two friends and I)

____

5 (tomorrow – you – to Italy – going – are – ?)

____

6 (Egypt – you – when – did – visit – ?)

____

B Write the story by putting the words and phrases into the right order.

0 (came – at 7.30 this morning – the postman)

The postman came at 7.30 this morning.

1 (he – a letter – brought)

____

2 (It – a letter from Maria and her son Matthew – was)

____

3 I – before I went to work – read – it)

____

4 (they – here – next week – are coming)

____

5 (at the airport – them – on Tuesday – I – am going to meet)

____

6 (at my house – are going to stay – they)

____

7 (takes – abroad – her son – every year – she)

____

8 (him – last year – took – she – to France)

____

9 (next year – her – am going to visit – I)

____

C Complete this job interview by putting in Mr Jones' questions.

Mr Jones: 0 Have you done this kind of work before?

Miss Smith: No, I haven't done this kind of work.

Mr Jones: Where 1 ______________ the advertisement?

Miss Smith: I saw it in the local newspaper.

Mr Jones: Do 2 ______________?

Miss Smith: No, I don't speak any foreign languages

Mr Jones: Where 3 ______________ at the moment?

Miss Smith: I'm working in a travel agent's at the moment.

Mr Jones: When 4 ______________?

Miss Smith: I started there two years ago.

Mr Jones: Can 5 ______________?

Miss Smith: Yes, I can use a computer.

Mr Jones: 6 ______________?

Miss Smith: Yes, I like the job.

Mr Jones: Why 7 ______________?

Miss Smith I'm leaving because I want to earn more money.

Mr Jones: 8 ______________?

Miss Smith: I can start next month.

19 **Who?** and **What?**: subject and object questions

1 Compare these examples:

SUBJECT
Ann: *Who* ***told*** *you?*
Mary: *James told me.*

This is a subject question.

OBJECT
Ann: *Who* ***did*** *you* ***tell****?*
Mary: *I told Bill.*

This is an object question.

2 Compare subject and object questions with **Who**:

In the sentence ***Who*** *told you?*, **Who** is the subject. Here is another example:

SUBJECT
Ann: *Who* ***wrote*** *Hamlet?*
(= **Somebody** wrote *Hamlet*. Who?)
Mary: *Shakespeare wrote Hamlet.*

When **Who** is the subject, the order of the words is the same as in a statement:

SUBJECT
Who ***is going*** *to come with me?*
Who ***lives*** *in that old house?*
Who ***wants*** *some more coffee?*

In the sentence ***Who*** *did you tell?*, **Who** is the object. Here is another example:

OBJECT
Ann: *Who* ***did*** *you* ***meet*** *last night?*
(= You met **somebody**. Who?)
Mary: *I met a couple of friends.*

When **Who** is the object, we use an auxiliary (**be**, **do**, **have** etc.) before the subject:

OBJECT
Who ***are*** *you* ***going*** *to invite?*
Who ***did*** *Laura* ***ask*** *for help?*
Who ***have*** *you* ***told*** *about this?*

3 Compare subject and object questions with **What**:

SUBJECT
What ***is*** *in this dish?*
(= **Something** is in it. What?)

OBJECT
What ***did*** *you* ***buy*** *at the shops?*
(= You bought **something**. What?)

Practice

A **Write questions beginning with *Who* or *What* from the sentences in brackets ().**

0 (Eric met **somebody**.) Who did Eric meet?
0 (**Somebody** ate the last piece of cake.) Who ate the last piece of cake?
1 (**Somebody** wants some more coffee.) ____________
2 (**Something** happened at the end of the story.) ____________
3 (**Somebody** is going to pay the bill.) ____________
4 (He had **something** for breakfast.) ____________
5 (Their letter said **something**.) ____________
6 (**Somebody** knows the answer to my question.) ____________
7 (They saw **something**.) ____________
8 (She is phoning **somebody**.) ____________

B Use the 'full' answers to write questions using *Who* or *What*. (We usually use the short, underlined answers when we reply to a question.)

QUESTIONS		ANSWERS
0 Who were you talking to on the phone?	~	(I was talking to) **Elizabeth** (on the phone).
0 What was the result of the game?	~	(The result of the game was) **2–0 to Italy**.
1 ______?	~	**Anita and Frank** (went on the trip).
2 ______?	~	**I'm not sure** (what's happening in this film).
3 ______?	~	(I'm going to phone) **Jane**.
4 ______?	~	(I watched) **that new comedy programme** (on TV last night).
5 ______?	~	**John** (sent these flowers).
6 ______?	~	(I bought) **a book** (in that shop).
7 ______?	~	**Some good news** (has made Tom so happy).

C Read this story and then complete the questions.

Two days ago Robert took his driving test. He failed it. Afterwards he met his friend Philip. He told Philip that he had failed his test. Then he said, 'Don't tell anyone. It's a secret.' Philip said, 'OK, I won't tell anyone.'

Later that day, Philip met Linda for coffee and he said, 'Robert failed his driving test.' Linda laughed. 'Poor Robert,' she said.

QUESTIONS		ANSWERS
0 (What / Robert / do / two days ago?) What did Robert do two days ago?	~	He took his driving test.
1 (What / happen?) ______	~	He failed it.
2 (Who / take / his / driving test?) ______	~	Robert.
3 (What / Robert / fail?) ______	~	His driving test.
4 (Who / Robert / meet / afterwards?) ______	~	He met Philip.
5 (What / Robert / say / to Philip?) ______	~	He said, 'Don't tell anyone.'
6 (What / Philip / say / to Robert?) ______	~	Philip said, 'OK, I won't tell anyone.'
7 (Who / Philip / meet / for coffee?) ______	~	He met Linda.
8 (What / Philip / say / to Linda?) ______	~	He said, 'Robert failed his driving test.'
9 (What / Linda / do?) ______	~	She laughed.

20 How long? How far? How often? How much? etc.

1 We use **How long ...?** to ask about a period of time:

How long have you been waiting? ~ About 20 minutes.
How long will the journey take? ~ Three hours.

We use **from ... to** or **from ... until** to talk about a period of time:

*She was a student **from** 1985 **to** 1990.*
*Tomorrow I'm working **from** 8.30 **until** 6.*

2 We use **How far ...?** to ask about the distance from one place to another. We can use **from** and **to** with the places we are asking about:

***How far** is it **from** Amsterdam **to** Paris? ~ 475 kilometres.*
***How far** are the shops **from** here? ~ Not far.*

3 We use **How often ...?** to ask about the number of times something happens. We can use phrases like **every day**, **once a week** etc. in the answer:

***How often** do the buses run? ~ **Every hour**.*
***How often** do you play squash? ~ **Twice a week**.*

4 We can use **How much ...?** to ask about the price of something:

***How much** is a return ticket to Florence?*
***How much** did you pay for this car?*

5 We use **How much ...?** with an uncountable noun to ask about the amount of something. An uncountable noun cannot be plural because it describes something that cannot be counted (e.g. **bread**, **work**, **weather**, **money**, **music**, **meat**, **milk**, **cheese**).

***How much bread** is there in the cupboard?*
***How much work** have you done today?*

6 We use **How many ...?** with a plural noun to ask about numbers:

***How many students** are in your class? ~ 15.*
***How many people** went to the party? ~ Ten.*

7 We use **How old ...?** to ask about someone's age:

***How old** are you? ~ I'm 19.*

Note that we say:

I am 19, or: *19*. (Not ~~*I have 19.*~~)

We can also say: *I'm 19 years old.*

But we cannot say: ~~*I'm 19 years.*~~

Practice

A **Complete the questions using *How long, How old, How often* etc. Put the verbs into the correct tense.**

QUESTIONS	ANSWERS
0 (How / you / stay / in New Zealand?) How long did you stay in New Zealand?	~ I stayed there for six months.
1 (How / he / read / a newspaper?) ______	~ He reads one every day.
2 (How / a single room / cost?) ______	~ It costs £50 a night.
3 (How / be / you when you went to live in Australia?) ______	~ I was 15 when I went there.
4 (How / exams / you / going to take?) ______	~ I'm going to take three exams.
5 (How / the course / last?) ______	~ It will last for two years.
6 (How / be / it from here to the nearest bus stop?) ______	~ It's about 200 metres.

B Make each question using the words in brackets ( ), and *How old*, *How much*, *How many* etc. Put the verbs into the correct tense.

0 A: How old is your husband ______ (your husband/be)?
B: He is 34. He'll be 35 next month.

1 A: ______ (languages you/speak)?
B: I speak three – English, French and Chinese.

2 A: ______ (it/be) from here to the airport?
B: It's about 25 kilometres.

3 A: ______ (the meal/cost)?
B: I can't remember, but it wasn't very expensive.

4 A: ______ (you/stay) there?
B: I stayed there from June until October.

5 A: ______ (the postman/come)?
B: He comes twice a day.

6 A: ______ (cheese/you/buy)?
B: I bought half a kilo.

C Complete each of these sentences by putting one word into each gap.

0 It was my birthday last week. I am ______ 21.
1 The programme lasts ______ 8.30 ______ 10 o'clock.
2 There is a train to the centre ______ 30 minutes in the morning.
3 How ______ money have you got?
4 How far is it ______ here ______ the city centre?
5 My grandfather is seventy ______ ______ .
6 How ______ countries have you visited?

D Complete the conversation by putting in Bob's questions. Start with *How …* each time.

Anne: I'm doing a course in computing.
Bob: Oh really. 0 How long have you been doing it ______ ?
Anne: I've been doing it for about a month. It's at the local college.
Bob: 1 ______ ?
Anne: I go there twice a week.
Bob: 2 ______ ?
Anne: The lessons last for three hours, from 2 o'clock until 5.
Bob: 3 ______ ?
Anne: I study at home every evening.
Bob: 4 ______ ?
Anne: There are about 25 people in my class.

Bob: 5 ______ ?
Anne: They're all about the same age as me.
Bob: 6 ______ ?
Anne It's not far from my home.
Bob: 7 ______ ?
Anne: It doesn't cost anything. My company is paying.

21 Question tags (**It's cold, isn't it?**)

1 A question tag is a short question (e.g. **isn't it?**, **haven't we?**) that we can add at the end of a statement:

Henry: *We've met before, **haven't we?***
Jeff: *Yes, we have.*

2 Look at this bit of a conversation:

Anna: *Sandra is Swiss.*
David: *No, she's French, **isn't she?*** ↗
(= I thought she was French, but am I wrong?)

When tag questions really are questions, like David's, the voice goes up at the end.

But when tag questions are not really questions, the voice goes down at the end:

*That was a boring programme, **wasn't it?*** ↘
(= I think that was a boring programme.)

3 Note that the verb we use in the tag depends on the verb used in the statement:

VERB	+ TAG	
be:	*You'**re** French,*	***aren't** you?*
verb:	*He **plays** golf,*	***doesn't** he?*
auxiliary verb:	*It **has** arrived,*	***hasn't** it?*

4 A positive statement has a negative tag:

POSITIVE +	NEGATIVE
***I'm** right,*	***aren't I?*** (Not ~~amn't I?~~)
***You're** 18,*	***aren't you?***
***They're** getting tired,*	***aren't they?***
***They were** friendly,*	***weren't they?***
***He lives** in France*	***doesn't he?***
***You speak** Spanish,*	***don't you?***
***You passed** your exams,*	***didn't you?***
***She has** left,*	***hasn't she?***
***You can** drive,*	***can't you?***
***The bus will** come soon,*	***won't it?***

5 A negative statement has a positive tag:

NEGATIVE +	POSITIVE
***It isn't** very cheap,*	***is it?***
***We aren't** going to be late,*	***are we?***
***She wasn't** angry,*	***was she?***
***You don't** like this,*	***do you?***
***She didn't** win,*	***did she?***
***She hasn't** visited Ireland,*	***has she?***
***She can't** drive,*	***can she?***
***It won't** rain today,*	***will it?***

Practice

A **Complete the conversation by putting in question tags.**

Tim: We haven't met before, [0] have we ?
Jo: No, I've just arrived in this country.
Tim: You come from Australia, [1] ________ ?
Jo: Yes, from Sydney.
Tim: It's very hot there, [2] ________ ?
Jo: Most of the time, but not always.
Tim: But it never gets very cold, [3] ________ ?
Jo: No, well, not as cold as some places.
Tim: They speak English there, [4] ________ ?
Jo: Yes, that's right.
Tim: You haven't been here long, [5] ________ ?
Jo: No, I only got here two weeks ago.
Tim: You're on holiday, [6] ________ ?
Jo: Yes, I'm travelling around for six months.

B Complete the sentences by putting in question tags.

0 The programme starts at 7 o'clock, doesn't it ? ~ Yes, that's right.

1 I can use this ticket on any bus, __________ ? ~ Yes, you can.

2 The bill won't be very high, __________ ? ~ No, I don't think so.

3 He wasn't very polite, __________ ? ~ No, he wasn't.

4 I didn't make a mistake, __________ ? ~ No, you didn't.

5 It won't be a difficult thing to do, __________ ? ~ No, I don't think so.

6 That was a lovely meal, __________ ? ~ Yes, it was delicious.

7 You can't play the piano, __________ ? ~ No, I can't.

8 They left last week, __________ ? ~ Yes, that's right.

C Complete the conversation with question tags.

Marta: I'm going to Helsinki tomorrow.

Charles: That's in Finland, [1] __________ ?

Marta: Yes, it's the capital.

Charles: You've been there before, [2] __________ ?

Marta: Yes, two years ago.

Charles: But you can't speak Finnish, [3] __________ ?

Marta: No, I can't.

Charles: But a lot of Finnish people speak English, [4] __________ ?

Marta: Yes.

Charles: Well, I'll see you before you leave, [5] __________ ?

Marta: Yes, I'll see you tonight.

D Complete the sentence with a question tag before each reply.

0 A: She comes from Italy, doesn't she?

B: Yes, she comes from Italy.

1 A: You can __________

B: Yes, I can speak French very well.

2 A: You haven't __________

B: No, I haven't heard this story.

3 A: You went __________

B: Yes, I went to Frank's party.

4 A: It isn't __________

B: No, it isn't very far from here.

5 A: She won't __________

B: No, she won't be angry.

6 A: You're not __________

B: No, I'm not going to leave now.

7 A: You'll __________

B: Yes, I'll be at home tonight.

22 Must, mustn't (I must leave)

1 We use **must** with an infinitive (**do**, **go**, **work**, etc.):

*You **must*** [INFINITIVE] ***work*** *harder.*

Don't use **to** before the infinitive:
Not ~~*You must to work harder.*~~

The form of **must** is the same for all persons:

I/you/he/she/it/we/they **must leave** soon.

2 We use **must** in rules, to say that an action is necessary:
*All visitors **must go** to reception when they arrive.*

We use **You must** ... to give somebody an order:
*Your work is poor – **you must try** harder.*
***You must finish** this work tomorrow.*

We use **I/We must** ... to say that we think it is necessary that we do something:
*I'm getting tired. **I must go** home now.*
***We must get** a new car soon.*

3 We also use **You must** ... to strongly recommend or offer something:
***You must read** this book; it's fantastic!*
***You must come** for lunch at our house.*

4 The negative form of **must** is **mustn't** or **must not**:
*You **mustn't park** here – it's not allowed.*
Not ~~*You mustn't to park here.*~~

5 We use **You mustn't** ... (or **You must not**) to say that it is necessary that somebody does NOT do something:
***You mustn't smoke** in here.*
***You mustn't make** this mistake again.*

We use **I/We mustn't** ... (or **must not**) to say that we think it is necessary that we do NOT do something:
***I mustn't forget** her birthday again.*
***We mustn't be** late for the meeting.*

6 Notice that we can use **must** and **mustn't** (not ~~*will must*~~) to talk about the future:
I must phone Harry tomorrow.
(Not ~~*I will must phone ...*~~)

To talk about what was necessary in the past, we cannot use **must**; we use a form of **have to** (see unit 23).

We don't generally use **must** in a question form. We use **have to** (see unit 23).

Practice

A The 'Hotel Strict' is not a very nice hotel. It has a lot of rules. Read the list of rules, and change each one into a sentence using *must* or *must not*.

Notice to guests
Leave your key at reception when you go out.
Do not take food into your room.
Pay for your room when you arrive.
Vacate your room by 9 a.m. on the day you leave.
Do not smoke in the restaurant.
Return to the hotel before 10 o'clock every night.

0 *You must leave* ________ your key at reception when you go out.
1 You ________ food into your room.
2 ________ for your room when you arrive.
3 ________ your room by 9 a.m. on the day you leave.
4 ________ in the restaurant.
5 ________ to the hotel before 10 o'clock every night.

B Complete the sentences with *must* or *mustn't* and the verb in brackets.

0 You must hear ______ (hear) this story; it's extremely funny!
1 We ______ (forget) to buy some petrol. There isn't much left.
2 I ______ (go) to the shops this afternoon. I've got no food in the house.
3 You ______ (worry) so much; it's bad for you.
4 We ______ (book) the tickets before it's too late.
5 You ______ (lock) the door with this key every time you go out.
6 You ______ (see) that new, French film. It's really good.
7 I ______ (phone) Jane tonight. She asked me to call her.

C Look at this table of instructions for students in a school. Use the table to make sentences with *must* or *mustn't*.

	Yes	No
Attend all classes.	✓	
Take school books home with you.		✓
Make a noise in the corridors.		✓
Write in school books.		✓
Arrive for lessons on time.	✓	
Bring your own pens and paper.	✓	

0 You must attend ______ all classes.
1 ______ school books home with you.
2 ______ a noise in the corridors.
3 ______ in school books.
4 ______ for lessons on time.
5 ______ your own pens and paper.

D Rewrite the sentences in brackets using *must* or *mustn't* / *must not*.

0 (Have some of this fish. It's wonderful.)
You must have some of this fish ______. It's wonderful.
1 (Don't tell lies. It's bad.)
You ______. It's bad.
2 (Passengers: Do not open the door while the train is moving.)
Passengers ______ while the train is moving.
3 (Come for dinner with us one evening next week!)
You ______ one evening next week!
4 (All staff: Show identity cards when you enter the building.)
All staff ______ when they enter the building.
5 (It's bad for you to eat so much unhealthy food.)
You ______ so much unhealthy food.
6 (Follow the instructions when using this machine.)
You ______ when using this machine.
7 (It's important that I write this letter today.)
I ______ this letter today.

23 Have to (He has to go)

1 The Present Simple forms of **have to** are:

POSITIVE & NEGATIVE

I/you/we/they	**have** / **don't have**	**to go.**
He/she/it	**has** / **doesn't have**	**to go.**

QUESTIONS

Do	I/you/we/they	**have**	**to go?**
Does	he/she/it	**have**	**to go?**

2 We use **have to** to talk about things that are necessary because of rules that other people oblige us to follow:

*My brother **has to travel** a lot in his job.* (It is required by his employer.)

*We **have to pay** the rent every month.* (It is required by the landlord.)

To talk about things that WE think are necessary, we usually use **must** (see unit 22).

3 We also use **have to** for things that are necessary because of the circumstances:

*I **have to get** a bus to school.* (It is the only way I can travel there.)

*She **has to live** on a small income.* (She only receives a small amount of money to pay for what she needs.)

4 We use **don't have to** to say that something is NOT necessary:

*We **don't have to hurry**; we're early.* (= It's not necessary to hurry. We have plenty of time.)

*I **don't have to get** up early on Sunday. I can stay in bed if I want.*

5 We form the past of **have to** like this:

*I **had to do** a lot of work yesterday.*

*We **didn't have to play** football at school.*

***Did** you **have to work** hard for the exam?*

6 We form the future of **have to** like this:

*He**'ll have to look** for another job.*

*We **won't have to get** tickets in advance.*

***Will** they **have to get** visas?*

Note that we can use the Present Simple of **have to** to talk about the future:

*I **have to do** some shopping tomorrow.*

***Do** you **have to work** next weekend?*

Practice

A Look at this table about different jobs and use the information to complete the sentences, using *have to* or *don't have to*.

	Shop Assistants	Bank clerks	Doctors	Teachers
deal with the public	✓	✓	✓	✗
be polite to people	✓	✓	✗	✗
work with money	✓	✓	✗	✗
wear uniforms	✓	✗	✓	✗

0 Shop assistants have to deal with ______ the public.
1 Teachers ______ the public.
2 Teachers ______ to people.
3 Bank clerks ______ to people.
4 Shop assistants ______ with money.
5 Bank clerks ______ with money.
6 Doctors ______ with money.
7 Shop assistants often ______ uniforms.
8 Teachers ______ uniforms.

B Complete the sentences using the correct forms of *have to* and the words in brackets. Be careful to use the correct tense.

0 I have to leave (I/leave) now; I've got an appointment at the dentist's.
0 Did you have to study (you/study) literature when you were at school?
0 You don't have to come (You/not/come) with me now if you don't want to.
1 ______ (I/not/work) hard because the job was very easy.
2 ______ (I/do) this work now, or can I do it tomorrow?
3 ______ (I/run) to school because I was late.
4 ______ (I/go) to an important meeting yesterday.
5 ______ (you/show) your passports when you reached the border?
6 ______ (I/pay) in cash next week or can I give you a cheque?
7 I want to be an airline pilot. What qualifications ______ (you/have) to be a pilot?
8 ______ (You/not/decide) today. You can tell me tomorrow.
9 I arrived late yesterday because ______ (I/wait) a long time for a bus.
10 A: ______ (you/work) every weekend?
B: No, I don't; but ______ (I/work) last weekend.

C Complete the conversations, using the correct forms of *have to*.

A: (Good morning, I'd like to buy a travel card. What / I / do?)
0 Good morning. I'd like to buy a travel card. What do I have to do?

B: (You / fill / in an application form.)
1 ______

A: (I/ give / you / a photograph?)
2 ______

B: (No, you / not / give / me anything, except the money for the card!)
3 ______

Dad: (What / you / do / at school today?)
0 What did you have to do at school today?

Geoff: (We / do / some / English tests.)
4 ______

Dad: (How many questions / you / answer?)
5 ______

Geoff: (We / answer / about 40 grammar questions.)
6 ______

(I / think / about them very carefully.)
7 ______

Dad: (you / write / a composition?)
8 ______

Geoff: (No, but we / do / one next week.)
9 ______

24 Should, shouldn't (You shouldn't smoke)

1 We use **should** with an infinitive (**do, go** etc.):

*I **should** **do** some work tonight.* (INFINITIVE: do)

The form of **should** is the same for all persons:

I/you/he/she/it/we/they **should go.**

2 The negative form is **shouldn't**:
*You **shouldn't sit** in the sun all day.*
*They **shouldn't spend** so much money.*

3 We use **I should** or **we should** to say what is a good thing for us to do:
*I **should go** home. It's midnight.*
*We **should invite** them for a meal.*

We use **I** or **we shouldn't** to say that something is a bad thing for us to do:
*I **shouldn't spend** so much money.*

We use **you should/shouldn't** to give advice:
*You **should look** for a better job.*
*You **shouldn't drive** so fast.*

Should is not as strong as **must** or **have to.** Compare:
*You **should eat** more fruit.* (It's a good idea.)
*'You **must eat** more fruit,' said the doctor.* (It's very important).

4 We use the question form **should I/we ...?** to ask for advice:

*What **should** I **say** to Helen?*
*I need a new passport. Where **should** I **go**?*

5 We can say **I think we should, I don't think you should** etc. to give an opinion:

***I don't think you should believe** everything he says.*
We do not usually say:
~~*I think you shouldn't ...*~~

6 We can use **do you think I should ...?** to ask for advice:
*He hasn't replied to my letter. **Do you think I should phone** him?*
*What **do you think** I **should give** Tom for his birthday?*

Practice

A Complete the sentences, using *should* or *shouldn't* and the words in brackets.

0 You shouldn't work (You/work) so hard. Have a holiday.
0 I enjoyed that film. We should go (We/go) to the cinema more often.
1 ________________ (You/park) here. It's not allowed.
2 What ________________ (I/cook) for dinner tonight?
3 ________________ (You/wear) a coat. It's cold outside.
4 ________________ (You/smoke). It's bad for you.
5 ________________ (We/arrive) at the airport two hours before the flight.
6 ________________ (I/pay) now or later?
7 Do you think ________________ (I/apply) for this job?
8 What do you think ________________ (I/write) in this space on the form?
9 ________________ (I/eat) any more cake. I've already eaten too much.
10 This food is terrible. ________________ (We/complain) to the manager.
11 Which shirt do you think ________________ (I/buy) ?

B Henry is cooking a meal. Give him some useful advice. Use *you should* or *you shouldn't* and the notes in the box.

Don't leave the meat in the oven for more than one hour. Cut the onions as small as possible. Use fresh herbs and fresh vegetables. Don't put in too much salt and pepper. Wait until the water boils before you put the vegetables into it. Heat the oven before you put the meat in. Cut the meat into four equal slices.

0 You shouldn't leave the meat in the oven for more than one hour.
1 ______________ the onions as small as possible.
2 ______________ fresh herbs and fresh vegetables.
3 ______________ in too much salt and pepper.
4 ______________ until the water boils before you put the vegetables into it.
5 ______________ the oven before you put the meat in.
6 ______________ the meat into four equal slices.

C Write this conversation between Brian and Keith using the words in brackets. Put in *do* or *should* where required.

Brian: (I want to buy a motorbike. What / you / think / I / do?)
0 I want to buy a motorbike. What do you think I should do?

Keith: (You / look / at the advertisements in the papers.)
0 You should look at the advertisements in the papers.

Brian: (Which papers / I / get?)
1 ______________

Keith: (I think / you / buy / the local newspapers.)
2 ______________

Brian: (What / you / think / I / do / before I buy a bike?)
3 ______________

Keith: (I / not / think / you / decide / too quickly.)
4 ______________

(You / check / the condition of the bike.)
5 ______________

(You / ask / somebody who knows about bikes to look at the bike for you.)
6 ______________

(You / not / buy / one simply because it looks nice!)
7 ______________

(You / be / very careful.)
8 ______________

25 Can, could; may, might

1 We use **can** or **could** with an infinitive (**do**, **speak**, **swim** etc.):

		INFINITIVE	
I/you/he (etc.)	***can***	***swim***	*to the island.*

2 Look at these examples with **can**:

> ABILITY:
> *I **can speak** four languages.*
> (= I am able to speak four languages.)
> ***Can** you **swim**?*
> (= Are you able to swim?)

We use **can** to talk about what people are able to do.

In the negative, we use **can't** or **cannot** to talk about what people are not able to do:
*Please speak slowly. I **can't** understand you.*
(= I am not able to understand you.)
*Robert **can't run** as fast as Sarah.*
*We **can't go** abroad for our holiday this year, because we **cannot afford** the air fare.*

We use **could** and **couldn't** to talk about what people were able to do in the past:
*When Jane was little, she **could swim** before she **could walk**.*
*I **couldn't answer** every question in the test.*
*I **couldn't go** to their party. I was ill.*

3 We use **may** or **might** with an infinitive (**do**, **go**, **leave** etc.):

		INFINITIVE	
I/you/he/we (etc.)	***may***	***leave***	*soon.*

4 Look at these examples with **may** and **might**:

> POSSIBILITY:
> *The letter **may come** tomorrow.*
> (= It's possible that the letter will come tomorrow.)
> *Ask Eric. He **might know** the answer.*
> (= Perhaps Eric knows the answer.)

We use **may** or **might** to talk about things that are possible, now or in the future.

The negative is **may not** or **might not**:
*I'll phone her, but she **may not be** at home.*
(= It's possible that she isn't at home.)
*I **might not go** to work tomorrow.* (= It's possible that I won't go to work tomorrow.)

Note that we can use the short form **mightn't**, but we do not say ~~**mayn't**~~:
*She **mightn't be** at home now.*
*I **mightn't go** to work tomorrow.*

Practice

A **Complete the sentences with *can, can't* or *couldn't* and the verbs in brackets ().**

0 You don't have to shout. I can hear (hear) you very well.
0 I couldn't watch (watch) that programme last night because I had to go out.
1 He ________________ (play) last week because he was injured.
2 He eats in restaurants all the time because he ________________ (cook) .
3 I ________________ (give) you a lift in my car because it isn't working at the moment.
4 I didn't have a good seat in the theatre, so I ________________ (see) the stage very well.
5 John doesn't need a calculator. He ________________ (do) very difficult sums in his head.
6 She's very good at music. She ________________ (play) three instruments.
7 I ________________ (find) my address book. Have you seen it?
8 He spoke very quickly and I ________________ (understand) anything he said.
9 We ________________ (go) on the trip because we ________________ (afford) it. It was very expensive.

10 I ____________ (do) any more work because I was very tired, so I stopped.

11 I'm afraid that I ____________ (talk) to you now. I'm in a hurry. I have to be at work in five minutes.

B Use the words in brackets to complete each sentence, with *can, can't, could* or *couldn't*.

0 Sarah phoned Jane yesterday. (They / not / talk / for a long time, because Jane had to go out.)
They couldn't talk for a long time, because Jane had to go out.

1 Grandma needs her glasses. (She / not / see / anything without her glasses.)
She ____________

2 Mary won her race. (She was so tired after the race that she / not / stand / up.)
She ____________

3 (Last year, Robert / beat / his younger brother at chess.) But he can't beat him now.
Last year, ____________

4 John and Anna have a wonderful view from their hotel room. (They / see / the whole of the city.)
They ____________

C Complete the sentences, using *might* or *might not* and the verb in brackets.

0 Accept their offer. You might not get (get) a better opportunity.

1 I ____________ (buy) her this plant for her birthday. She likes plants a lot.

2 Take a coat with you. It ____________ (be) cold this evening.

3 We ____________ (go) to Greece this summer, but we haven't booked anything yet.

4 I ____________ (go) by car because there will be a lot of traffic.

5 They ____________ (come) to the party tonight. They're very busy. They have a lot of things to do at home.

6 A: What are you going to do tonight?
B: I'm not sure. I ____________ (stay) at home. I'm tired.

7 I know Jane is at school today. But I don't know where she is at the moment. She ____________ (be) in the gym, or she ____________ (be) in the science lab.

8 Don't worry too much about that mistake. It ____________ (be) important.

9 I'll try to change the time of my flight, but it ____________ (be) possible. The planes are often full at this time of year.

10 You ____________ (find) a good hotel if you go to the main street — there are lots of hotels there.

D Complete the conversation using *may* or *may not* and the verbs in brackets.

Jane: Are you going to the concert tomorrow?
Chris: I [0] may go (go), but there [1] ____________ (be) any tickets left.
Jane: What will you do if you can't go to the concert?
Chris: I'm not sure. I [2] ____________ (go) out at all. I [3] ____________ (stay) at home. I [4] ____________ (watch) a video.
Jane: What kind of film will you get?
Chris: I don't know. I [5] ____________ (get) a horror film. I like them!

26 Passive: Present Simple and Past Simple

1 We form the Present Simple passive like this:

	am/is/are + PAST PARTICIPLE	
Glass	***is***	***made*** *from sand.*

POSITIVE & NEGATIVE

This programme ***is shown*** *on TV every Thursday.*

These computers ***aren't produced*** *any more.*

QUESTIONS

When ***is*** *breakfast* ***served*** *in this hotel?*

(For information on the forms of regular past participles, see Table D on page 95, and for irregular past participles, see Table E on page 96.)

2 We form the Past Simple passive like this:

	was/were + PAST PARTICIPLE	
Anna	***was***	***born*** *in Germany.*

POSITIVE & NEGATIVE

'Romeo and Juliet' ***was written*** *by Shakespeare.*

The goods ***weren't delivered*** *yesterday.*

QUESTIONS

When ***was*** *your camera stolen?*

3 Look at these sentences:

		OBJECT	
ACTIVE:	*They sell*	*cold drinks*	*here.*
PASSIVE:	*Cold drinks* (SUBJECT)	*are sold here.*	

Notice that the object in the active sentence (**cold drinks**) is the same as the subject in the passive sentence. We use the passive when it is not important who does the action, or when we don't know who does it:

These cars are made in Japan. (We don't need to say ~~*... by Japanese workers.*~~)

This castle was built in the twelfth century. (We don't know who built it.)

4 Now look at these examples:

(i) ***Alfred Hitchcock*** *was a great film maker.* ***He*** *directed this film in 1956.*

(ii) *This is a wonderful* ***film. It*** *was directed by Alfred Hitchcock.*

In (ii) we use the passive because we have been talking about something (**the film**), and not the person who did it (**Hitchcock**). We use **by** to say who does, or did, the action:

This film was directed ***by Hitchcock.***

Practice

A Complete these sentences with the Present Simple passive form of the verbs in brackets ( ).

0 English _is spoken_ (speak) in many countries.

1 The post ________ (deliver) at about 7 o'clock every morning.

2 Dinner ________ (serve) in the hotel at 8.30 p.m.

3 The building ________ (not/use) any more.

4 The Olympic Games ________ (hold) every 4 years.

5 How ________ (your name/spell) ?

6 What kinds of things ________ (sell) in that market?

7 My salary ________ (pay) every month.

8 These computers ________ (make) in Japan.

9 The rubbish ________ (take) away three times a week.

10 The name of the person who committed the crime ________ (not know) .

11 This programme ________ (show) three times a week.

12 His travel expenses ________ (pay) by his company.

B Complete these sentences using the Past Simple passive form of the verbs in brackets.

0 My car was repaired (repair) last week.
1 This song ____________ (write) by John Lennon and Paul McCartney.
2 The phone ____________ (answer) by a young girl.
3 The film ____________ (make) ten years ago.
4 When ____________ (tennis/invent) ?
5 She ____________ (not/injure) in the accident.
6 He ____________ (be born) in 1965.
7 Where ____________ (this pot/make) ?
8 When ____________ (this city/build) ?
9 This picture ____________ (paint) by Picasso.
10 When ____________ (this book/publish) ?
11 The money ____________ (give) to him by his parents.

C Change the active sentences into passive sentences. Use the words in brackets.

0 We sell tickets for all shows at the Box Office.
(Tickets for all shows / sell / at the Box Office) Tickets for all shows are sold at the Box Office.
1 Thomas Edison invented the electric light bulb
(The electric light bulb / invent / by Thomas Edison) ____________
2 Someone painted the office last week.
(The office / paint / last week) ____________
3 Several people saw the accident.
(The accident / see / by several people) ____________
4 Where do they make these video recorders?
(Where / these video recorders / make) ____________
5 Six countries signed the agreement.
(The agreement / sign / by six countries) ____________
6 A stranger helped me.
(I / help / by a stranger) ____________
7 They don't deliver the post on Sundays.
(The post / not / deliver / on Sundays) ____________

D Put in the correct active or passive form in brackets ( ).

Fiat

Fiat [0] was started (started/was started) by a group of Italian businessmen in 1899. In 1903, Fiat [1] ____________ (produced/was produced) 132 cars. Some of these cars [2] ____________ (exported/were exported) by the company to the United States and Britain. In 1920, Fiat [3] ____________ (started/was started) making cars at a new factory at Lingotto, near Turin. There was a track on the roof where the cars [4] ____________ (tested/were tested) by technicians. In 1936, Fiat launched the Fiat 500. This car [5] ____________ (called/was called) the Topolino – the Italian name for Mickey Mouse. The company grew, and in 1963 Fiat [6] ____________ (exported/was exported) more than 300,000 vehicles. Today, Fiat is based in Turin, and its cars [7] ____________ (sold/are sold) all over the world.

27 Verb + -ing (I like cooking); like and would like

1 Look at this example:

	-ing FORM	
*I **like***	***listening***	*to music.*

(For details on **-ing** forms, see Table C on page 95.)

We can use certain verbs (e.g. **like**) with an **-ing** form:

like	**enjoy**	**love**	**keep**	+ **-ing** FORM
finish	**stop**	**mind**		

*She doesn't **like cooking**.*
*Do you **enjoy driving**?*
*They **love living** in a village.*
*He **keeps saying** the same things.*
(= He says the same things many times.)
*Have you **finished eating**?*
*Suddenly she **stopped talking**.*
*I don't **mind waiting**.*

2 Compare this pair of sentences:

> *I **like** working here.*
> (= I enjoy my job here.)
> ***I'd like** (= I would like) to get a better job.*
> (= I want to get a better job.)

We use **like** + **-ing** (e.g. **like listening**, **like working**) to talk about things that we enjoy doing. We use **would like to** to say that we want to do something. Here are some more examples:

*She **likes painting** pictures.*
(= She enjoys painting pictures.)
*She **would like to be** an artist.*
(= She wants to be an artist.)

*I **like going** to the theatre.*
(= I enjoy going to the theatre.)
***I'd like to go** to the theatre tonight.*
(= I want to go to the theatre tonight.)

*Do you **like playing** cards?*
(= Do you enjoy playing cards?)
***Would** you **like to play** cards now?*
(= Do you want to play now?)

In offers and requests it is more polite to say **would like** than **want**:

***Would** you **like to come** for dinner?* (offer)
***I'd like to leave** work early, please.* (request)

3 We use **go** + **-ing** for sports and hobbies that we go out to do, and with **shopping**:

*We often **go skiing** in the winter.*
*Let's **go swimming** this afternoon.*
*She **goes dancing** at weekends.*
*I'm **going shopping** this afternoon.*

Practice

A Complete the sentences using a Present Simple form of the first verb in brackets. Study the example first.

0 She likes playing ______ (like/play) tennis, but she doesn't like watching ______ (not/like/watch) it.
1 The buses ____________ (stop/run) at midnight.
2 I ____________ (not/mind/listen) to his problems.
3 He's not very good at playing chess, so he ____________ (keep/lose).
4 She ____________ (enjoy/go) to other countries and she ____________ (like/meet) new people.
5 I ____________ (keep/make) the same stupid mistakes!
6 They usually ____________ (finish/eat) at about 8.30 in the evening.
7 She ____________ (not/enjoy/drive), but she ____________ (love/cycle).
8 ____________ (you/like/read) detective novels?
9 I ____________ (not/mind/change) the time of our appointment.
10 Please ____________ (stop/make) that terrible noise!

B Complete the sentences using ***like/not like* + *-ing*** or ***would like* + *to*** with the words in brackets.

0 She _doesn't like working_ (work) here. She hates this job and is going to look for a better one.

0 _Would you like to watch_ (you / watch) a different programme, or do you want to watch this one?

1 I ________________ (live) here. I have lived here for many years and I think it's a nice town.

2 Sarah ________________ (be) a journalist when she leaves university. She wants to work on a newspaper or a magazine.

3 I ________________ (get up) so early every morning, but I have to do it.

4 I ________________ (go out) for dinner in an Italian restaurant tonight.

5 Clare ________________ (find) a job in the United States. She wants to work in Boston or in New York.

6 I ________________ (watch) television all the time; I think it's a waste of time.

7 Mary ________________ (lie) on the beach when she's on holiday. She doesn't like swimming or going on trips.

8 I ________________ (discuss) something important with you this afternoon.

9 ________________ (you/come) to a party at my house next Saturday?

10 I ________________ (do) nothing this weekend — I'm very tired.

11 Jane ________________ (go) to parties; she always enjoys them.

12 Bruce ________________ (cook), so he often eats in restaurants.

13 A: Susan is working as a secretary in an office in the centre of London.
B: ________________ (work) in an office?
A: No, she hates it. She ________________ (find) a different job.

14 A: What ________________ (you/do) next summer?
B: I ________________ (visit) South America, but I might not have enough money.

C Look at the pictures. They show what John did last week on holiday. Complete the sentences using the correct form of *go* and a verb from the box.

dance
~~shop~~
sail
swim
ski
cycle

0

Monday

1

Tuesday

2

Wednesday

3

Thursday

4

Friday

5

Saturday

0 On Monday _he went shopping._
1 On Tuesday ________________
2 On Wednesday ________________
3 On Thursday ________________
4 On Friday ________________
5 On Saturday ________________

28 To + infinitive (**I want to go**) or infinitive (**I can go**)

1 Look at this example:

	to + INFINITIVE	
*I **want***	***to buy***	*some stamps.*

We use **to do, to buy, to start** etc. (**to** + infinitive) after these verbs:

want	**decide**	+ **to** + INFINITIVE
agree	**promise**	
forget	**offer**	
hope	**plan**	
arrange	**try**	

*She **agreed to lend** him some money.*
*He **forgot to book** the tickets.*
*I'm **hoping to get** a new bike soon.*
*I've **arranged to play** tennis tonight.*
*They've **decided to start** a new company.*
*You **promised to help** me.*
*She **offered to do** the washing-up.*
*We're **planning to go** away this weekend.*
*He's **trying to learn** French.*

2 We can also say **want** + someone + **to**:
*His parents **want him to go** to university.*
*Do you **want me to help** you?*

3 Now look at this example:

	INFINITIVE	
*He **can***	***speak***	*Spanish.*

Can is a modal verb. We use **do, speak, see** etc. (infinitives) after a modal verb. Some of the most common modal verbs are:

will ('ll) should may	+ INFINITIVE
might can could must	

***I'll see** you soon.*
*She **won't agree**.*
*Where **should** I **sit**?*
*We **may go** by train.*
*It **may not cost** much.*
***Can** I **park** here?*
*I **couldn't hear** her.*
*We **must pay** now.*

4 We can use **make** + someone + **infinitive**, to mean 'cause' or 'force':
*The film **made me cry**.*
(= It caused me to cry.)
*They **made us leave**.*
(= They forced us to leave.)

5 We can use **let** + someone + **infinitive**, to mean 'allow':
*She **let me stay**.* (= She allowed me to stay.)

Practice

A Put the verbs in brackets ( ) into these sentences. Use an infinitive (*phone*) or *to* + infinitive (*to phone*).

0 You can't smoke __________ (smoke) here. Smoking is not allowed in this building.
1 I'm sorry I forgot __________ (phone) you yesterday. I was very busy.
2 Don't worry. The exam may not __________ (be) very difficult.
3 My boss makes me __________ (work) very hard.
4 It's not a very good film. You won't __________ (enjoy) it.
5 She didn't want __________ (wait) any longer, so she left.
6 When are you planning __________ (eat) tonight?
7 She couldn't __________ (reply) because she didn't know what to say.
8 This kind of music makes me __________ (feel) good.
9 Our boss sometimes lets us __________ (leave) early.
10 I'm afraid I've forgotten __________ (bring) the map.
11 They might not __________ (receive) the letter until next week.

B Complete each sentence so that it has the same meaning as the sentence in brackets.

0 (I don't think it's a good idea to argue with him.)
I don't think you should argue with him.

1 (I won't be able to come to the meeting on Friday.)
I can't ______

2 (I'm meeting some friends tonight.)
I've arranged ______

3 (Listen to what I'm telling you.)
I want you ______

4 (It's important that you lock the door when you go out.)
Don't forget ______

5 (Perhaps we'll go out for a meal this evening.)
We may ______

6 (Allow me to pay for the meal.)
Let ______

7 (I'd like to do a course in Art History.)
I want ______

8 (He said, 'I'll pay the bill'.)
He offered ______

9 (Should I sit in this chair?)
Do you want me ______?

10 (His stories were very funny, and I laughed a lot.)
His funny stories made ______

11 (Perhaps he'll phone you tomorrow.)
He might ______

12 (It's possible that Tom won't be angry with you.)
Tom might not ______

13 (Jane allowed me to drive her new car.)
Jane let ______

C Complete the conversation, using the verbs in brackets with or without *to*.

Charles: I want [0] to do (do) something interesting this weekend. Can we [1] ______ (do) something together?

Diana: Well, I've arranged [2] ______ (go) on a trip to the coast with some friends. Do you want [3] ______ (come) with us?

Charles: Yes, that sounds good. When are you planning [4] ______ (leave) ?

Diana: Well, we've decided [5] ______ (start) early in the morning tomorrow, and I've promised [6] ______ (take) the others in my car. We're hoping [7] ______ (reach) the coast by lunchtime. So, you must [8] ______ (meet) me here at 6.30 a.m.

Charles: Okay, good. I won't [9] ______ (be) late.

29 Reported speech; **say/said** or **tell/told**

1 When we report something that somebody said, we usually change the tense of the verb like this:

ACTUAL WORDS	REPORTED SPEECH
Present Simple *'I live in a small flat,' she said.*	→ Past Simple *She said she **lived** in a small flat.*
Present Continuous *'I'm leaving on Tuesday,' I said.*	→ Past Continuous *I said that I **was leaving** on Tuesday.*
Past Simple Present Perfect *'I learnt a lot,' he said.* *'Mr Jackson has left,' she said.*	→ Past Perfect *He said he **had learnt** a lot.* *She said that Mr Jackson **had left**.*
will *'I'll help you,' she said.*	→ **would** *She said she **would help** me.*
am/is/are going to *'We're going to be late,' I said.*	→ **was/were going to** *I said that we **were going** to be late.*
can *'I can't find my money,' he said.*	→ **could** *He said he **couldn't** find his money.*

2 Note that it is not necessary to use **that** in reported speech:

*She said (**that**) she knew the answer.*

3 Compare **say** and **tell** in these sentences:

*She **said** (that) she lived in a small flat.*
*She **told me** (that) she lived in a small flat.*

We **say something**. We do not **say someone something**.

She said she was going to be late.
(Not ~~*She said **me** she was …*~~)
I said that I disagreed with him.
(Not ~~*I said **him** that I …*~~)

We **tell someone something**. We do not **tell something**.

*He told **me** he was happy.*
(Not ~~*He told he was happy.*~~)
*He told **me** that he would pay me immediately.*
(Not ~~*He told that he would pay me immediately.*~~)
*She told **Fred** she was going to meet someone.*
(Not ~~*She told that she was going to meet someone.*~~)

Practice

A Look at these pictures of people coming through passport control at an airport. Change the things they said into reported speech.

0 

1 

2 

3 

4 

5 

0 He said that he was visiting friends.
1 She said ______________________
2 He said ______________________
3 They said ______________________
4 She said ______________________
5 They said ______________________

B **Read this conversation and then report what Claudia and Nicole said.**

Nicole: How long have you been in France?
Claudia: Six weeks.
Nicole: Are you enjoying your stay?
Claudia: Yes, I'm enjoying it a lot.
Nicole: Have you been here before?
Claudia: Yes. I've been to France many times.
Nicole: What are you doing here?
Claudia: I'm on holiday.
Nicole: Are you staying in a hotel?
Claudia: No, I'm staying with some friends.
Nicole: Where do they live?
Claudia: They have a flat in the city centre.
Nicole: How long are you staying?
Claudia: I'm leaving in March.
Nicole: Can you speak French very well?
Claudia: No, I can't. I'm going to have some lessons.
Nicole: I'll teach you.

0 Claudia said that she had been __________ in France for six weeks.
1 Claudia said __________ her stay a lot.
2 Claudia said __________ to France many times.
3 Claudia said __________ on holiday.
4 She said __________ with some friends.
5 She said __________ a flat in the city centre.
6 She said __________ in March.
7 She said __________ French very well.
8 She said __________ some lessons.
9 Nicole said __________ Claudia.

C **Complete the sentences with *said* or *told*.**

0 She said __________ she wasn't feeling very well.
1 Alex __________ me that he would buy the tickets.
2 They __________ that the train was going to be late.
3 She __________ him that she was very angry with him.
4 She __________ him that she couldn't help him.
5 Who __________ you that I was leaving? It's not true!
6 They __________ us that they were leaving in the morning.
7 He __________ that he didn't know what was wrong with the car.
8 She __________ she had four sisters.
9 She __________ me that Tom worked in a factory.
10 He __________ me that he was a doctor, but he __________ Anna that he was a dentist.

30 Articles: a/an, the, or no article

1 We use **a/an** with singular nouns:
*He was reading **a book**.*

We use **an** before vowel sounds (**a,e,i,o,u**):
***an** apple* ***an** interesting film*
***an** hour* (pronounced 'our')

2 Now look at this example:
*When I arrived, John was reading **a book**.*

We use **a/an** when it isn't necessary to make clear which particular thing we are talking about. There are lots of books; John was reading one of them.

We use **a/an** to talk about people's jobs:
*Jim is **an engineer**.* (= There are lots of engineers; Jim is one.)

We use **a/an** to describe things or people:
*They have **a beautiful house**.* (= There are lots of beautiful houses; they have one.)
*John is **an old friend** of mine.*

3 We use **the** with singular or plural nouns:
***the** book* ***the** books*

We can use **the** with uncountable nouns (e.g. **music, water, food, education**):
***The water** is in the fridge.*

Note:
- ▶ uncountable nouns do not have a plural (not ~~2 musics~~, ~~three waters~~).
- ▶ we do not use **a/an** with uncountable nouns (not ~~a music~~, ~~a water~~).

4 We use **the** when it is clear which person or thing we are talking about:
*Jean was reading **a book**. She closed **the book**.* (= She closed the book that she was reading.)
*Anna likes music, but she doesn't like **the music** that John plays.*
*Mike's gone to **the shops**.* (= the local shops)
*She's in **the kitchen**.* (= the kitchen in this house)
*I must go to **the bank**.* (= my bank, where I keep my money)
the centre/the station/the airport (in a city)
the River Thames (There is only one.)
***the government** in my country*

5 We do not use **the** before plural nouns (e.g. **vegetables**) or uncountable nouns (e.g. **education, music**) when we are talking about something in general:
*Do you like **vegetables**?* (= any vegetables)
*I think **education** is very important.*

6 We do not use **a** or **the** before names of languages, meal names, the names of cities, most countries and most streets, and the names of airports, stations, single mountains or lakes:
*She speaks **Spanish**.*
*She lives in **Amsterdam** in **Holland**.* (But we say ***the** U.S.A., **the** United Kingdom.*)
*What time will **lunch** be?*
*from **Heathrow Airport** to **Oxford Street***

Practice

A Put *a, an* or *the* into the gaps if they are required. Leave the gaps empty if nothing is required.

0 I want to put some money into my bank account, so I'm going to __the__ bank this afternoon. It's in __–__ Midland Street.
1 I had ________ sandwich for ________ lunch today.
2 We flew to ________ Dublin Airport in ________ Ireland.
3 It was ________ long flight, but eventually we arrived in ________ U.S.A.
4 I'm trying to learn ________ Japanese. I'm having ________ lesson tomorrow.
5 He made ________ angry speech against ________ government.
6 She is ________ famous actress and she is appearing in ________ popular TV series.
7 They live in ________ Paris in ________ area near to ________ River Seine.
8 They've bought ________ small flat in ________ Park Street.

B **Complete the sentences by putting in *a, an* or *the* if required. Leave the gap empty if nothing is required. (Note that the following words in this exercise are uncountable nouns: *music, fuel, education, fish, food, coffee, exercise.*)**

0 She read the______ letters that had arrived that morning.

1 It was a nice day, so we had ________ lunch in ________ garden of my house.

2 I'm just going to ________ shops. I'll be back in a few minutes.

3 We phoned for ________ taxi to take us to ________ airport.

4 I like listening to ________ music when I come home.

5 Without ________ fuel, ________ cars don't work.

6 John was at home. He was reading ________ magazine in ________ living-room.

7 His parents believe that ________ education is a very important thing.

8 Jane doesn't like ________ fish; she never eats it.

9 After ________ dinner, I washed ________ plates and glasses.

10 Did you like ________ food at ________ party yesterday?

11 A: Where's ________ coffee?

B: It's in ________ cupboard next to ________ sink.

12 Doctors say that ________ exercise is good for everybody.

C **Complete this conversation by putting in *a, an* or *the* if required. Leave the gap empty if nothing is required.**

Mike: Is Maria 0 a______ student at your college?

Rosie: No, she's 1 ________ old friend of mine. We were at school together.

Mike: What does she do now?

Rosie: She's 2 ________ computer programmer. She's not English, you know. She comes from 3 ________ Brazil, but she's living in 4 ________ U.S.A. at the moment.

Mike: Has she got 5 ________ job there?

Rosie: Yes, she's working for 6 ________ big company there.

Mike: Do you write 7 ________ letters to each other?

Rosie: Yes, and I had 8 ________ long letter from her yesterday.

Mike: What did she say in 9 ________ letter?

Rosie: She said that she was living in 10 ________ nice apartment in 11 ________ centre of 12 ________ Chicago.

D **Complete the story by putting *a, an* or *the* into the gaps.**

Yesterday I was sitting on 0 the______ 6 o'clock train when I saw 1 ________ strange man walking along the platform. He came into the carriage of 2 ________ train where I was sitting, and he sat in the seat opposite mine. He opened 3 ________ newspaper and started reading it. On 4 ________ front page of 5 ________ newspaper, there was 6 ________ picture of 7 ________ bank robber. The words under 8 ________ picture were: 'Wanted by the police'. It was 9 ________ same man!

31 Myself, yourself etc; each other

1 Look at this table:

SUBJECT PRONOUNS	OBJECT PRONOUNS	REFLEXIVE PRONOUNS
I	me	myself
you (*singular*)	you	yourself
he	him	himself
she	her	herself
it	it	itself
we	us	ourselves
you (*plural*)	you	yourselves
they	them	themselves

2 Compare:

(i)

Jenny made Jo a cup of coffee.
(= Jenny made the coffee for Jo.)

(ii)

*Jenny made **herself** a cup of coffee.*
(= Jenny made the coffee for herself.)

We use **myself, yourself, herself** etc. to refer to the subject:

SUBJECT

*Be careful. **You** might hurt **yourself**.*

*I bought **myself** a new shirt.*
*He taught **himself** to swim.*
*They enjoyed **themselves** at the concert.*

3 We also use **myself, yourself** etc. to emphasize that the subject did the action, not another person:
*He built the whole house **himself**.*
(= He built it alone; nobody helped him.)

4 We use **each other** like this:
*Tom and Sue were talking to **each other**.*
(= Tom was talking to Sue, and Sue was talking to Tom.)
*We like **each other** very much.* (= I like her and she likes me.)

Compare **themselves** and **each other**:
*Alan and Ruth took these photographs **themselves**.* (= They took them, not another person.)
*Alan and Ruth took photographs of **each other**.* (= Alan took a photograph of Ruth, and Ruth took a photograph of Alan.)

Practice

A Fill the gaps with *myself, yourself* etc.

0 I cooked myself a meal and then I watched television.
1 I'm sure he'll enjoy ______________ on his trip.
2 I cut ______________ while I was preparing the vegetables.
3 We amused ______________ by playing cards while we were waiting for the plane.
4 She put the plates on the table and told them to help ______________ to the food.
5 Tom hurt ______________ when he was playing football.
6 Alan cooked ______________ a snack when he got home.

B Complete the sentences with the correct verb tenses and *myself, yourself* etc. in the correct place.

0 (Be careful with that knife or you / cut /.)
Be careful with that knife or you'll cut yourself.
1 (It was a very nice trip and we / enjoy / very much.)
It was a very nice trip and we ______________________________

2 (I / burn / while I was taking the dish out of the oven.)

I ________________ while I was taking the dish out of the oven.

3 (He didn't have lessons. He / teach /.)

He didn't have lessons. ________________

4 (I think I / buy / a new coat tomorrow.)

____

5 (She / make / a sandwich and ate it in the kitchen.)

________________ and ate it in the kitchen.

C Fill the gaps with *myself, yourself* etc.

0 Did you paint the room yourself? ~ Yes, it took me three days to do it.

1 If you won't help me, I'll have to do it all ________ .

2 She makes all her clothes ________ .

3 The students organized the concert ________ .

4 We painted the whole house ________ .

5 He typed the letter ________ and then he posted it.

D Complete the sentences with the correct verb tenses and *myself, yourself* etc. Put *myself, yourself* etc. at the end of the sentence.

0 (She is a very successful singer. She / write / all her songs /.)

She is a very successful singer. She writes all her songs herself.

1 Could you post this letter for me? ~ (No, I'm sorry, I won't have time. You / have / to post it /.)

No, I'm sorry, I won't have time. ________________

2 (Nobody helped us, so we / carry / all our luggage /.)

Nobody helped us, so ________________

3 (This is an excellent photograph. / you / take it /?)

This is an excellent photograph. ________________

4 (She was wearing a dress that she / make /.)

She was wearing a dress that ________________

5 (I hope you like the present. I / choose / it /.)

I hope you like the present. ________________

6 (Do you like this meal? I / invent / the recipe /.)

Do you like this meal? ________________

E Fill the gaps with *each other, ourselves, yourselves* or *themselves.*

0 They spent the whole evening arguing with each other.

0 Their house is very beautiful; they designed it themselves.

1 Mary met John in April, but they didn't see ________ again until July.

2 They're not friends; in fact, they don't like ________ at all.

3 Don't ask me to help you. You must do it ________ .

4 We didn't buy it ________ . A friend bought it for us.

5 I could hear two people shouting at ________ .

6 We're working in the same office now, so Ron and I see ________ every day.

32 Direct and indirect objects (**She gave him a book**)

1 Look at this example:

(i) *She gave* ***her brother*** *the newspaper.*
(ii) *She gave the newspaper* ***to her brother.***
In both sentences **a newspaper** is the thing which is given, and **her brother** is the person who receives it.

2 Here are other sentences like (i) *She gave* ***her brother*** *the newspaper*:

	+ PERSON (indirect object)	+ THING (direct object)
She ***gave***	*her brother*	*a shirt.*
He ***sent***	*me*	*a letter.*
I ***showed***	*him*	*my passport.*
Jane ***lent***	*Frank*	*some money.*
I'll ***offer***	*her*	*a job.*
I'll ***cook***	*them*	*a meal.*
I ***fetched***	*her*	*a plate.*
I'll ***get***	*you*	*a magazine.*
I'll ***buy***	*you*	*a coffee.*

3 Here are some other sentences like (ii) *She gave the newspaper* ***to her brother***:

	+ THING (direct object)	+ PERSON (**to** + object)
She ***gave***	*a shirt*	***to*** *her brother.*
I ***sent***	*postcards*	***to*** *my friends.*
I ***showed***	*my card*	***to*** *the clerk.*
She ***lent***	*some money*	***to*** *her friend.*
He ***offered***	*the chocolates*	***to*** *the others.*

Note that we use **to** + object after these verbs which express the idea of giving or showing something to somebody:
give, send, show, lend, offer

But we use **for** + object after verbs which express the idea of doing something for another person:
cook, fetch, buy, get (= 'fetch' or 'buy')

	+ THING (direct object)	+ PERSON (**for** + object)
We ***cooked***	*a meal*	***for*** *everybody.*
He ***fetched***	*the newspaper*	***for*** *his father.*
I'll ***get***	*your book*	***for*** *you.*
She ***bought***	*some toys*	***for*** *them.*

Practice

A Put these words into the right order to make sentences. Do not add any words.

0 (He – lent – his car – Mark)
He lent Mark his car.

1 (a cigarette – Jim – She offered)

2 (Mary – his holiday photographs – He showed)

3 (them – an invitation – Have you sent – ?)

4 (a birthday present – Did you buy – her – ?)

5 (I – some of my tapes – a friend – gave)

6 (When you go to the post office, – some stamps – me – could you get – ?)

B Now write the sentences from Exercise A again, but using *to* or *for*.

0 He lent his car to Mark.
1 She offered ______
2 He showed ______
3 Have you sent ______
4 Did you buy ______
5 I gave ______
6 When you go to the post office, could you get ______

C Change these sentences. In each case use the other possible structure.

0 He offered his seat to an old lady.
He offered an old lady his seat.
1 I have sent Jane a birthday card.
______
2 I don't want to lend my bike to Bruce.
______
3 I gave your message to Joan.
______
4 Could you fetch me a knife and fork?
______

D Tim and Lucy went to a restaurant last night for a meal. Make sentences about what happened while they were there. Write two sentences. Use the words in brackets ( ).

0 (The waiter / give / the menu.)
(her) The waiter gave her the menu.
(to Lucy) The waiter gave the menu to Lucy.
1 (The waiter / fetch / some wine.)
(them) ______
(for them) ______
2 (The waiter / show / the bottle.)
(him) ______
(to Tim) ______
3 (The chef / cook / a special meal.)
(them) ______
(for them) ______
4 (The waiter / give / the bill.)
(Tim) ______
(to Tim) ______
5 (Lucy / lend / some money, because he didn't have enough to pay the bill.)
(Tim) ______
(to Tim) ______

33 something, anybody, nothing etc.

1 **something / anything** = a thing
somebody / anybody = a person
someone / anyone = a person
somewhere / anywhere = a place

2 We usually use **something, somebody, someone** and **somewhere** in positive sentences:
__Something__ is burning. (= I can smell burning. I don't know what is burning.)
I'm going to have __something__ to eat. (= I'm going to eat; I don't know what I'm going to eat.)
__Somebody__ told me that it was a good film. (= A person told me it was a good film. I can't remember who told me.)
She lives __somewhere__ in the north.

3 We usually use **anything, anybody, anyone** and **anywhere** in negative sentences, and in questions:
I didn't know __anyone__ at the party. (= There were no people at the party who I knew.)
I couldn't find my bag __anywhere__. (= I couldn't find my bag in any place.)
Did you understand __anything__ she said?

4 **nothing** = not anything
nobody = not anybody
no one = not anyone
nowhere = not anywhere

We use **nothing, nobody, no one** and **nowhere** before or after positive verbs:
__Nothing makes__ Joe unhappy. (= There isn't anything that makes Joe unhappy.)
There__'s nothing__ I want to watch on TV.
__Nobody was__ there when I arrived.
There __is nowhere__ that I would prefer to live than here. (= There isn't anywhere . . .)

5 We can use **else** after **something, anybody, nowhere** etc:
Let's talk about __something else__. (= Let's talk about a different subject.)
I didn't tell __anybody else__. (= I didn't tell another person.)
There is __nowhere else__ I can look for it.

6 We can also use an adjective (e.g. **wrong, nice**) after **something, anything** etc:
Have I said __something wrong__?

Practice

A Put in the correct word from the box in each gap.

anything (×2)	nobody (×2)	~~somebody~~	somewhere (×2)
nothing (×3)	something	anywhere	

0 Somebody__________ phoned you today, but he didn't tell me his name.
1 Everybody was having lunch in the restaurant, so there was ______________ in the office.
2 She didn't say ______________ about her job when I spoke to her.
3 I'm sure you'll find it ______________ if you keep looking.
4 I had to go to the cinema on my own because ______________ wanted to go with me.
5 A: Are you worried about something?
B: No, ______________ is worrying me.
6 Can I speak to you for a moment? I want to discuss ______________ with you.
7 Unfortunately, I couldn't help. There was ______________ I could do about the problem.
8 A: What did you buy at the shops?
B: I bought ______________. I couldn't find ______________ that I liked.
9 A: Have you seen my handbag ______________?
B: Yes, I think it's ______________ in the living-room.

B Choose the correct verb form in brackets.

0 I'm afraid I don't know ________ (know/don't know) anything about this subject.

0 I rang the doorbell but nobody was ________ (was/wasn't) in.

1 I asked a lot of people, but nobody ________ (knew/didn't know) the answer.

2 I ________ (have seen/haven't seen) anything so lovely before in my life!

3 I ________ (ate/didn't eat) anything for lunch yesterday.

4 Nothing interesting ________ (has happened/hasn't happened) since the last time I spoke to you.

5 He loves football. Nothing else ________ (is/isn't) important to him.

6 She ________ (said/didn't say) anything about her plans for the future.

C Change each of these sentences into a sentence with the same meaning. Use the word in brackets with the underlined adjective or with *else*.

0 A **strange** thing happened yesterday. (something)
Something strange ________ happened yesterday.

0 Let's listen to some different music. (something)
Let's listen to something else ________.

1 Is there an **interesting** programme on TV tonight? (anything)
Is there ________ on TV tonight?

2 You won't find better food in any other place. (anywhere)
You won't find better food ________.

3 Is there a **cheap** place we can go for lunch? (anywhere)
Is there ________ we can go for lunch?

4 Let's sit in a different place. (somewhere)
Let's sit ________.

5 I'd like a **hot** drink. (something)
I'd like ________ to drink.

D Put the right form of a word beginning with *some-*, *any-* or *no-* into the conversation.

Dennis: Have you read [0] anything ________ interesting lately?

Sarah: Yes, [1] ________ lent me a novel last week and I really enjoyed it.

Dennis: What was it about?

Sarah: It was about [2] ________ who goes to visit Australia. A few days after she arrives there, [3] ________ terrible happens to her.

Dennis: What?

Sarah: While she is travelling across Australia, she loses her passport and all her money. She doesn't know [4] ________ who can help her, and she hasn't got [5] ________ to stay.

Dennis: What happens then?

Sarah: I'm not going to tell you [6] ________ else! You should read the book yourself.

Dennis: It sounds like a very depressing book! I don't think I'll read it.

Sarah: You would like it. [7] ________ wonderful happens at the end.

34 All, most, some, none

1 We use

all/most/some + NOUN (e.g. **most cities**)

to talk about things or people in general:

*She thinks that **all sports** are boring.*
(= She thinks that **every sport** is boring.)
***Most cities** have a lot of shops.*
(= **Almost every city** has a lot of shops.)
*In **some countries** life is very hard.*
(= In a number of countries in the world, but not **all** or **most** ...)

We do not say **all/most/some** + **of** + noun:

***Most people** take exams during their lives.*
(Not ~~*Most of people ...*~~)

2 We can also use **all** with **morning/afternoon/evening/night/day/week/year** (e.g. **all afternoon**) to mean 'the whole', 'from the beginning to the end of':

*They've been working hard **all day**.*

*I waited for the phone call **all morning**.*

3 We use

all/most / **some/none** } + **of** + **the/my/her** + NOUN (e.g. **all of my books**)

to talk about particular things or people:

*He spent **all of his money**.*
*Most of **my friends** are interested in sport.*
*I knew **some of the people** at the party.*
***None of the shops** were open.*

Notice that we use a positive verb with **none**.

We can leave out **of** after **all** (but not after **most**, **some**, **none**):

*He spent **all his money**.*

4 We can use

all/most/some/none + **of** + **it/them**

when we have already mentioned the noun that **it** or **them** refers to:

*It was lovely food, but I couldn't eat **all of it**.*
(**it** = the food)
*I phoned a number of hotels, but **most of them** were full.* (**them** = the hotels)
*That cake looks nice. Can I have **some of it**?*
(**it** = the cake)

Practice

A **Look at these exam results for four people and complete the sentences, using *all of*, *some of*, *most of* or *none of*. Sometimes you will need *the* (e.g. *some of the*).**

Student	Exam 1	Exam 2	Exam 3	Exam 4	Exam 5	Exam 6
Alice	PASS	PASS	FAIL	PASS	PASS	PASS
Bill	PASS	PASS	PASS	PASS	PASS	PASS
Carol	FAIL	PASS	PASS	PASS	FAIL	FAIL
David	FAIL	FAIL	FAIL	FAIL	FAIL	FAIL

0 Alice passed <u>most of the</u> exams.
1 Bill passed ________________ exams.
2 Bill failed ________________ them.
3 Carol passed ________________ exams.
4 Carol passed ________________ them.
5 Carol failed ________________ them.
6 David passed ________________ them.
7 David passed ________________ exams.
8 David failed ________________ exams.

B Complete the sentences by putting in the correct words from the box.

all	some	all the	some of the	none of the

0 All __________ children have to go to school in this country by law.

0 The classroom was empty because all the __________ children had gone home.

1 We couldn't buy anything because __________ shops in the area were closed.

2 A: Where were you at 3 o'clock yesterday afternoon?

B: I was at home. I was at home __________ afternoon. I didn't go out until the evening.

3 We went to a restaurant last night. __________ food was lovely, but I didn't like the soup or the dessert.

4 __________ people say that he's the best tennis player in the world, but a lot of others don't agree.

5 It was a very boring day. __________ places that we visited were interesting.

6 He spent __________ morning reading the newspaper, so he didn't do any work.

7 __________ phones in the station worked, so I couldn't phone you.

8 We left the hotel at 9 o'clock in the morning, and we didn't go back to the hotel until the evening. We walked round the city, looking at the sights, __________ day.

9 __________ jackets fitted me, so I didn't buy one.

10 __________ passengers must buy a ticket before they travel.

11 She was ill. She stayed in bed from Monday to Saturday. She didn't go to work __________ week.

12 The teacher asked a question, but __________ students knew the answer, so the teacher told them.

13 __________ course was difficult for me, but most of it was easy.

C Complete the sentences by putting in the correct words from the box.

all of	all of it	most of them
most of	all of them	none of it
none of	most of it	none of them

0 I watched most of __________ the programme, but I didn't watch all of it __________.

1 I've read __________ the book, but I haven't read __________ yet. I'm reading the last chapter.

2 She did __________ the decorating herself, but she didn't do __________. A friend helped her with some of it.

3 A: Did you understand __________ the words in that story?

B: No, but I understood __________. There were only a few that I didn't know.

4 I rang __________ the hotels in the town, but __________ had vacant rooms, so we had nowhere to stay.

5 __________ the pens on my desk work; __________ are empty. Can I borrow yours?

6 I did __________ the work that I had to do. I finished at midnight. It took me a very long time to do it, because __________ was easy.

35 Both (. . . and), either (. . . or), neither (. . . nor)

1 We use **both**, **either** and **neither** to talk about two things or people. Look at this example with **both** ...**and**:

***Both** the white jumper **and** the black jumper are nice. He doesn't know which one to buy.*

We can also say:
***Both jumpers** are nice.*

2 Now look at this example with **either** ... **or**:

*Jeff would like to visit **either** Australia **or** India, but he can't decide which one.*

We can also say:
*Jeff **would like** to visit **either country**.*

We can also use a negative verb with **either**:
*Jeff **hasn't been** to **either** country.*

3 Now look at this example:

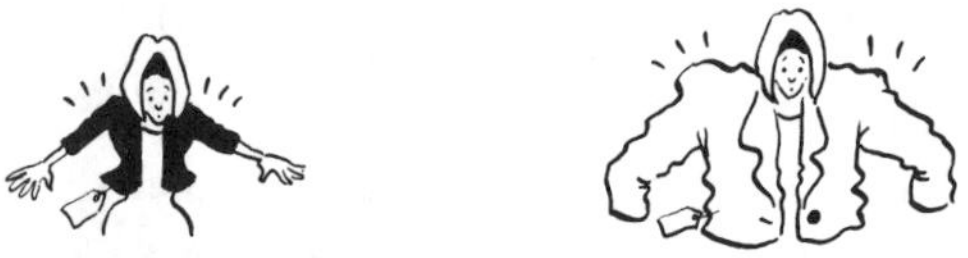

***Neither** the black jacket **nor** the white jacket fitted her.*

Or we can say:
***Neither jacket** fitted her.*

Note that we do not use a negative verb with **neither**:
Not ~~*Neither jacket didn't fit her.*~~
~~*Jeff hasn't been to neither country.*~~

4 We can also use **both**, **either**, and **neither** like this:

both **either** **neither**	**of**	**the** **my** **his** **these**	PLURAL NOUN

***Both of these suitcases** **are** heavy.* (PLURAL VERB)

*I haven't seen **either of the films.***

***Neither of his sisters** **was/were** there.* (SINGULAR or PLURAL VERB)

We can also say:

both/either/neither + of + them/us

*He has two cars, but **neither of them** works.*

Practice

A **Fill the gaps with *either* or *neither*.**

0 I'm going to buy <u>either</u> the green shirt or the blue shirt.
1 She lent me two books, but I haven't read ________ of them.
2 John looked at Jim, but they didn't speak. ________ of them said anything.
3 ________ of the two jobs seemed very attractive, so I didn't apply for ________ of them.
4 You can have ________ fish or chicken for dinner.
5 There were two films on TV, but ________ of them looked very interesting.
6 I haven't seen ________ James or Julie this week, and ________ of them has phoned me.
7 I looked for my bag in the living-room and in the kitchen, but it wasn't in ________ room.
8 I rang two friends, but ________ of them was at home. They had gone out.
9 You can catch ________ the number 12 bus or the number 15 bus to the city centre.

10 She didn't get ________ of the jobs she applied for.

11 I asked two people, but ________ of them could give me directions.

12 We can see the film ________ tonight or tomorrow night.

B Look at this information about two hotels. Then complete the sentences about them using *both of them* or *neither of them.*

	Grand Hotel	Landmark Hotel
It has a swimming pool.	✓	✓
It is in the city centre.	✓	✓
I t costs more than £100 a night.	✗	✗
It offers lower prices at weekends.	✓	✓
It organizes tours of the city.	✗	✗
It accepts credit cards.	✓	✓
It meets guests at the airport.	✗	✗

0 Both of them have swimming pools.

1 ________ are in the city centre.

2 ________ costs more than £100 a night.

3 ________ offer lower prices at weekends.

4 ________ organizes tours of the city.

5 ________ accept credit cards.

6 ________ meets guests at the airport.

C Complete the sentences using *both/either/neither* + *of* + *us/them* (e.g. *neither of us*).

0 I went to the concert with Mary, but neither of us enjoyed it very much because it was very boring.

1 There are two flights we can catch to New York. Both flights cost the same amount, so we can choose ________ .

2 I played two games against Harry, and I lost ________ because he is a much better player than me.

3 I saw Jane and Alison walking down the street and I waved at them, but ________ saw me because they were talking.

4 I looked at George, and George looked at me. Then ________ started to laugh because it was such a funny situation.

5 A man spoke to us but ________ could understand him, so we didn't answer.

6 Tim and I wanted to go to the game, but ________ could get tickets, so we watched it on TV.

7 I wanted to buy a new camera. There were two cameras in the shop that I liked, but they were very expensive. I couldn't afford ________ , so I didn't buy anything.

8 Ann and I worked very hard all day. ________ were very tired in the evening, so we didn't go out.

9 We went into two restaurants, but ________ were full. We couldn't get a table at either.

36 Comparative and superlative adjectives (**cheaper, cheapest**)

1 We use comparatives (e.g. **cheaper than**) to say that two or more things or people are different in some way:

Flights	
Geneva	£300
Zurich	£250

*The flight to Zurich is **cheaper than** the flight to Geneva.*
*The flight to Geneva is **more expensive than** the flight to Zurich.*

*It's **warmer** today **than** it was yesterday.*
*Is New York **bigger than** London?*

2 We use superlatives (e.g. **the cheapest**) like this:

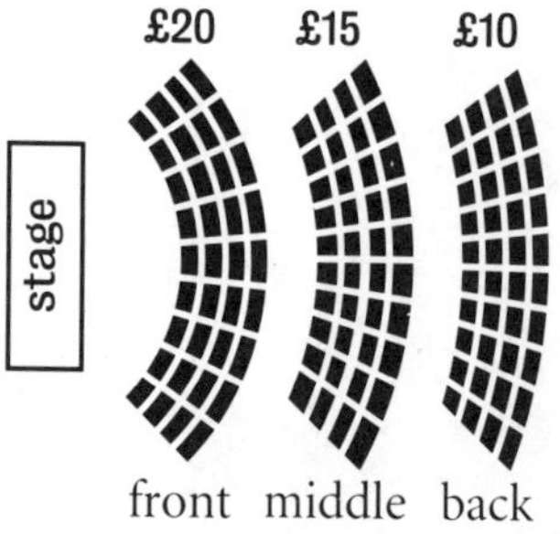

***The most expensive** seats are at the front of the theatre.*
***The cheapest** seats are at the back.*

*He is **the worst** player in the team.*
*It was **the happiest** day of their lives.*

We can use a superlative without a noun:
*The seats at the back are **the cheapest**.*

3 Look at these tables:

▶ short adjectives (1 syllable):

warm	warm**er**	the warm**est**
tall	tall**er**	the tall**est**
low	low**er**	the low**est**
big	bigg**er**	the bigg**est**
hot	hott**er**	the hott**est**
wet	wett**er**	the wett**est**

▶ long adjectives (2 syllables or more):

famous	**more** famous	the **most** famous
beautiful	**more** beautiful	the **most** beautiful

▶ adjectives ending with **-y**:

easy	eas**ier**	the eas**iest**
happy	happ**ier**	the happ**iest**

▶ irregular adjectives:

good	**better**	the **best**
bad	**worse**	the **worst**

(For more details see Table F on page 97.)

4 The opposite of **more** is **less**:
*The big book is **more expensive** than the little one.*
*The little book is **less expensive** than the big one.*

Practice

A **Look at the information about Alison and Bernard, and complete the sentences using the comparative form of the adjective in brackets ( ) and *than*.**

	Alison	Bernard
Height:	1.6m	1.75m
Age:	30	26
Income:	£15,000 per year	£70,000 per year
Family:	2 brothers and 2 sisters	1 brother
House:	small	very big

0 Alison is shorter than (short) Bernard.
1 Bernard is ______________ (tall) Alison.
2 Alison is ______________ (old) Bernard.
3 Bernard is ______________ (rich) Alison.
4 Alison's income is ______________ (low) Bernard's.
5 Alison's family is ______________ (big) Bernard's.
6 Alison's house is ______________ (small) Bernard's.

B Complete the sentences using the comparative form of the adjective in brackets and *than*.

0 I think that golf is more interesting than ______ (interesting) tennis.
1 This question is ____________ (easy) the last one.
2 I'm a good player, but Eric is ____________ (good) me.
3 The group's first record was ____________ (successful) their second record.
4 We both played well, but he was ____________ (lucky) me.
5 Your car is ____________ (powerful) mine.
6 This computer is ____________ (useful) that one.

C Complete the sentences using the superlative form of the adjective in brackets.

0 Anna is the youngest ______ (young) person in her class.
1 We stayed in ____________ (bad) hotel in the whole city.
2 People say that it is ____________ (funny) film of the year.
3 What is ____________ (tall) building in the world?
4 Her teachers say that she is ____________ (good) student in the school.
5 This is ____________ (expensive) camera in the shop.
6 Many people say that Venice is ____________ (beautiful) city in the world.

D Complete the dialogues using the comparative form of the adjective in brackets + *than*, or the superlative form of the adjective in brackets.

0 A: Why did you choose that hotel? It's a long way from the centre of town.
B: I chose it because it was cheaper than ______ (cheap) the hotel in the centre.
0 A: Shall we sit in the living-room?
B: Yes, it's the warmest ______ (warm) room in the house.
1 A: Did you enjoy being a student?
B: Yes, it was ____________ (happy) period of my life.
2 A: Is he famous in this country?
B: Yes, he's ____________ (famous) any other singer.
3 A: I'm not a very good cook.
B: I'm sure I'm ____________ (bad) you. I can't cook anything well.
4 A: Do you like this programme?
B: Yes, I think it's ____________ (good) programme on TV.
5 A: What did you have for dinner?
B: I chose ____________ (expensive) dish on the menu.
6 A: How is your new course going?
B: It's ____________ (difficult) the last one I took.
7 A: What's the weather going to be like today?
B: They say that today is going to be ____________ (wet) yesterday.
8 A: Are you happy in your new flat?
B: Yes, it's ____________ (comfortable) my last one.
9 A: Is London ____________ (exciting) city in Britain?
B: No, I think that Liverpool is ____________ (exciting) London.

37 Comparison: as . . . as (as strong as)

1 We use **as** + adjective + **as** (e.g. **as old as**) to say that two things or people are the same in some way:

*The chair is **as expensive as** the table.*

*You're **as old as** me.* (= We are the same age.)

Note that we say **as me / as him / as her / as us / as them**, and not **as I / as he / as she** etc:
*She's as strong as **him**.* (Not ~~*... as he.*~~)
*I'm as fast as **them**.* (Not ~~*... as they.*~~)

We use **not as . . . as** to talk about a difference between two things or people:

*The two star hotel is**n't as big as** the four star hotel.*

*I'm **not as clever as** her.* (= She is cleverer than me.)

2 We can also use **as** + adverb + **as** (e.g. **as well as**):
*Jean cooks **as well as** Tom.* (= Jean and Tom are both good cooks.)
*He couldn't run **as quickly as** Maria.* (= Maria ran more quickly than him.)

3 We use **as many** + plural noun + **as** (e.g. **as many friends as**) to say that the number of two things are equal:
*Jane has got **as many friends as** Mary.*

We use **not as many ... as** to say two things are not equal:
*I **don't** have **as many books as** you.*

4 We use **as much** + uncountable noun + **as** (e.g. **as much money as**) to compare two things. Uncountable nouns are words for things that we cannot count, and so they do not have a plural form (e.g. **money**, **work**, **luggage**, **traffic**):
*Helen earns **as much money as** Colin.*
*Jack doesn't do **as much work as** me.*
*They aren't carrying **as much luggage as** us.*

Practice

A Complete each sentence so that it means the same as the one above it. Use *as* + adjective/adverb + *as*.

0 Sweden is bigger than Britain.
Britain isn't as big as Sweden.

1 The other students learn more quickly than me.
I don't learn ______________ the other students.

2 You're very angry and I'm very angry also.
I'm ______________ you.

3 The seats at the front are more expensive than the seats at the back.
The seats at the back aren't ______________ the seats at the front.

4 Central Park in New York is bigger than Hyde Park in London.
Hyde Park in London isn't ______________ Central Park in New York.

5 Her last film was very good and her new film is also very good.
Her new film is ______________ her last film.

6 The other students work harder than him.
He doesn't work ______________ the other students.

B **Complete the sentences about each picture, using *as ... as* and a word from the box. Use each word once.**

long	clean	fast	fresh	tall
big	~~cheap~~	strong	wide	full

0

1

2

3

4

5

6

7

8

9

0 The carrots aren't as cheap as ______ the cabbages.
1 The black car is going ______ the white car.
2 The footballers aren't ______ the basketball players.
3 Janet's hair is ______ Kathy's hair.
4 The car on the left isn't ______ the car on the right.
5 The flowers on the right aren't ______ the flowers on the left.
6 The big glass isn't ______ the little glass.
7 Jane is ______ Matthew.
8 High Street isn't ______ Main Street.
9 The black book is ______ the white book.

C **Join each pair of sentences in brackets ( ), using *as much ... as* or *as many ... as.***

0 (I've got about 50 books. Jack's got about 100.)
I haven't got as many books as ______ Jack.
0 (You've done a lot of work. I've done a lot of work also.)
I've done as much work as ______ you.
1 (Alan earns a lot of money. Sheila only earns a little.)
Sheila doesn't earn ______ Alan.
2 (George has been to five countries. I've also been to five countries.)
I've been to ______ George.
3 (You've had five jobs. I've only had two.)
I haven't had ______ you.
4 (Tom has a lot of luggage. Jane has a lot of luggage too.)
Jane has ______ Tom.
5 (Mary answered most of the questions. I only answered about half.)
I didn't answer ______ Mary.
6 (Ruth spent £50. I also spent £50.)
I spent ______ Ruth.

38 Too and **enough** (**too big, big enough**)

1 Look at this example:

The case is ***too big****. He can't carry it.*
We use **too** to mean 'more than is good or suitable in the situation'.

2 We can use **too** like this:

too + ADJECTIVE: *I don't want to go out. I'm* ***too tired****.*
too many + PLURAL NOUN: *I couldn't find her at the concert because there were* ***too many people*** *there.*
too much + UNCOUNTABLE NOUN: (e.g. **too much work/money/food/noise/salt/information/time/bread**) *Our teacher gives us* ***too much work****.*

3 We can use **too** with **to** + infinitive to explain why someone cannot do something:
She's ***too*** *young* ***to drive****.* (= She can't drive because she's too young.)

4 Now look at this example:

This case is ***big enough****. I can put all my clothes into it. The small case* ***isn't big enough****.*
We use **enough** to mean 'as much or as many as we need'. We use **not ... enough** to mean 'less than we need'.

5 We can use **enough** like this:

ADJECTIVE + **enough:** *Is your room* ***warm enough?***
enough + PLURAL NOUN: *I've got* ***enough potatoes****, thanks.*
enough + UNCOUNTABLE NOUN: *I can't talk to you now. I haven't got* ***enough time****.*

6 We can also use **not ... enough** + **to** + infinitive to say why someone cannot do something:
She ***isn't old enough to drive****.* (= She can't drive because she isn't old enough.)

Practice

A Complete the sentences using *too* or *enough* and the word in brackets ( ).

0 I can't eat this soup because it's too hot (hot).
0 We couldn't buy the tickets because we didn't have enough money (money).
0 We didn't buy the car because it wasn't big enough (big).
1 I couldn't see her because it was ______________ (dark).
2 I can't decide what to do because I haven't got ______________ (information).
3 You can't change the situation now. It's ______________ (late).
4 Have you had ______________ (food), or would you like some more?
5 He did badly in the exam because he was ______________ (nervous).
6 Slow down! You're driving ______________ (fast).
7 He shouldn't play in the team because he isn't ______________ (good).
8 I haven't got ______________ (clothes). I must buy some more.
9 Robert didn't go to work because he didn't feel ______________ (well).
10 I couldn't lift the suitcase because I wasn't ______________ (strong).
11 We didn't go swimming because the water was ______________ (cold).
12 Mary couldn't post all the letters because she didn't have ______________ (stamps).

B Complete the sentences using *too much, too many* or *enough* and the word in brackets.

0 I'm not enjoying my job at the moment because they're giving me too much work (work).

0 Is your coffee sweet enough (sweet)?

1 Shall we have another coffee? Have we got ______________ (time)?

2 I couldn't finish the exam because there were ______________ (questions).

3 We didn't go for a walk because it wasn't ______________ (warm).

4 I couldn't eat the meal because there was ______________ (salt) in it.

5 Mary passed the test because she answered ______________ (questions) correctly.

6 I didn't enjoy the party because there were ______________ (people) there.

7 Is that chair ______________ (comfortable) or would you like to sit here?

8 George couldn't work because the others were making ______________ (noise).

9 We can't play that game because we haven't got ______________ (players).

10 Shall I make some sandwiches? Have we got ______________ (bread)?

11 Her work isn't very good. She makes ______________ (mistakes).

C Join each pair of sentences using *too* or *enough* with *to* + infinitive (e.g. *to do, to go*).

0 Clare couldn't sleep. She was too worried.
Clare was too worried to sleep.

0 I can't go on holiday. I haven't got enough money.
I haven't got enough money to go on holiday.

1 I can't do any more work. I'm too tired.
____

2 Judy won't pass the exam. She isn't good enough.
____

3 Clive can't play basketball. He's too short.
____

4 His girl-friend couldn't go to the party. She was too ill.
____

5 David couldn't pay the bill. He didn't have enough money.
____

6 Shall we go to the beach? Is it hot enough?
____

7 I can't see you tonight. I'm too busy.
____

8 I don't want to go home. It's too early.
____

9 Chris couldn't repair the car. He didn't have enough tools.
____

10 I didn't visit all the museums. I didn't have enough time.
____

39 Adjectives: -**ed** or -**ing** (**frightened** or **frightening**)

1 Compare **frightened** and **frightening**:

We can use adjectives that end with -**ed** to describe people's feelings:

SUBJECT
Ann *was very **frightened**.*

The subject of the sentence (e.g. **Ann**) is the person who has the feeling.

We use an adjective that ends with -**ing** (e.g. **frightening**) to talk about a thing or person that makes us have a feeling:

SUBJECT
The ghost *was very **frightening**.*

The subject of the sentence (e.g. **the ghost**) causes the feeling.

2 Here are some more examples to compare:

*We are all **surprised** by the news.*
(= We feel surprised.)
*I was very **tired** at the end of the journey.*
(= I felt tired.)
*He was **excited** by the way the game ended.*
*I'm **interested** in your idea.*
*The students were **bored** during the lesson.*
*Were you **disappointed** by the film?*
*I wasn't nervous before the exam; I was **relaxed**.*

*The news is **surprising**.*
(= The news makes us feel surprised.)
The journey was very **tiring**.
(= The journey made us feel tired.)
*The end of the game was **exciting**.*
*Your idea is **interesting**.*
*The lesson was **boring**.*
*Was the film **disappointing**?*
*I went for a **relaxing** walk.*

Note that we can say:
*The **journey** was very **tiring**.*
or:
*It was a very **tiring journey**.*

Practice

A Choose the correct adjective in brackets ( ) to put in the gaps.

0 It was a terrible play and I was *bored* ______ (bored/boring) from start to finish.
1 I'm very ______ (excited/exciting) because I'm going to New York tomorrow.
2 Are you ______ (surprised/surprising) or were you expecting this news?
3 I'm reading a very ______ (interested/interesting) book at the moment.
4 I've had a very ______ (tired/tiring) day at work today and I want to go to bed.
5 Most people were ______ (surprised/surprising) that he won the championship.
6 I'm ______ (bored/boring). Let's go out for a cup of coffee somewhere.
7 Visit our ______ (excited/exciting) new shop!
8 His speech was very long and very ______ (bored/boring).

B Complete each sentence using the correct word from the box. Use each word once.

bored	interested	surprising	amusing	confused
boring	amused	confusing	surprised	~~interesting~~

0 Your idea is very _interesting_________ . Tell me more about it.

1 He told me a very ____________________ story. I laughed and laughed.

2 This is a terribly ____________________ book. Nothing happens in it.

3 She's ____________________ in politics and often talks about it.

4 The map was ____________________ and I got lost.

5 She was ____________________ because she had nothing to do all day.

6 Everyone else thought it was funny, but she wasn't ____________________ .

7 Could you repeat that, please? I'm a bit ____________________ because it was very complicated.

8 It is ____________________ that she failed the exam, because she's a good student.

9 Everyone was ____________________ by the sudden noise.

C Complete the replies in these dialogues, using the correct word from the box.

confused	boring (x2)	surprised	disappointed
bored	disappointing (x2)	~~confusing~~	surprising

0 A: Do you understand what's happening in this film?
B: No, it's very _confusing_________ .

1 A: Did you think the film was good?
B: No, I was ____________________ from the beginning to the end. I nearly fell asleep.

2 A: Was your trip to London as good as you expected?
B: No, it was rather ____________________ . I didn't like the place. People had told me that London was beautiful, but I thought it was dirty and ugly.

3 A: Did you enjoy your course?
B: No, I was ____________________ because I thought I would learn more.

4 A: Do you enjoy your job?
B: No, it's very ____________________ . I do the same things every day.

5 A: Did you know that he was going to leave his job?
B: No, I was very ____________________ . I had no idea he was planning to do that.

6 A: Do you understand the rules of this game now?
B: No, I'm completely ____________________ .

7 A: Were you expecting him to get so angry?
B: No, it was very ____________________ . He's usually very calm about everything.

8 A: I'm sorry to hear that you failed the exam.
B: Yes, it was very ____________________ . I really wanted to pass.

9 A: Do you like watching golf on TV?
B: No, I think it's very ____________________ . Nothing happens for long periods of time.

40 Adverbs (**slowly, fast**); comparative adverbs (**more quickly**)

1 Compare adverbs and adjectives:

ADVERBS We use adverbs (e.g. **beautifully**) to describe how someone or something does an action: *Peter **plays** the violin **beautifully**.* (**Beautifully** describes how Peter plays.)
ADJECTIVES We use adjectives (e.g. **beautiful**) to describe people or things. We use adjectives before nouns, or after **be/seem/get**: *Look at that **beautiful violin**!* *That violin **is beautiful**.*

2 We form most regular adverbs by adding **-ly** to the adjective:

slow → slowly **bad → badly**

*The whole team played very **badly**.*
*She answered all the questions **correctly**.*

If an adjective ends with **-y**, the adverb ends with **-ily**:

happy → happily **easy → easily**

*We solved the problem **easily**.*

If an adjective ends with **-ble**, the adverb ends in **-bly**:

comfortable → comfortably

3 Some adverbs are irregular; they do not end with **-ly**:

good → well

*He's a **good** guitar player.* (**good** = adjective)
*He plays the guitar **well**.* (**well** = adverb)

Fast and **hard** are both adjectives and adverbs:

fast → fast **hard → hard**

*Maria is a **fast** learner.* (**fast** = adjective)
*Maria learns **fast**.* (**fast** = adverb)
*James is a **hard** worker.* (**hard** = adjective)
*James works **hard**.* (**hard** = adverb)

4 We form the comparative of regular adverbs with **more**:

carefully → more carefully

*You should do your work **more carefully**.*

The comparative of **well** is **better**:
*She speaks Arabic **better** than me.*

The comparatives of **fast** and **hard** are **faster** and **harder**:
*Could you walk **faster**? We're in a hurry.*
*You will have to work **harder** in future.*

Practice

A **Put in the adjective or the adverbs in brackets ( ).**

0 The train was very slow __________ (slow/slowly) and I arrived late.
1 The journey took a long time because the train went very __________ (slow/slowly).
2 Mrs Green went __________ (quick/quickly) back to her office.
3 I'm afraid I can't give you an __________ (immediate/immediately) answer; I need to think about it first.
4 The work that the builders did for us was very __________ (bad/badly).
5 The builders did the work for us very __________ (bad/badly).
6 She organized the party very __________ (good/well), and everybody enjoyed it.
7 Everybody said that the party was very __________ (good/well).
8 She wrote a __________ (polite/politely) letter asking the company to give her the money back.
9 She wrote to the company and asked them __________ (polite/politely) to give her the money back.

B Complete the sentences. Put in the adverb form of the adjective in brackets ( ).

0 She read the message _quickly_ (quick).
1 Read the instructions ______ (careful).
2 He looked at her ______ (angry), but he didn't say anything.
3 She passed all her exams ______ (easy).
4 I ran as ______ (fast) as I could.
5 He thinks that he did the test ______ (bad) and that he'll fail.
6 I've been studying very ______ (hard) recently.
7 She was working ______ (busy) when I arrived.
8 She sang the song ______ (beautiful).
9 He was playing ______ (happy) when I came into the room.
10 He was concentrating ______ (hard) on his work.
11 Have I filled this form in ______ (correct)?
12 I wasn't in a hurry, so I walked ______ (slow) through the park.
13 I closed the door ______ (quiet) when I left.

C Complete the dialogues by putting a suitable adverb into the gaps. Use an adjective from the box to make the adverb.

slow	fast	hard	good (x2)	~~easy~~	bad

0 A: Were the questions difficult?
B: No, I answered them _easily_.
1 A: Does she speak English ______ ?
B: No, she only knows a few words of English.
2 A: Hurry up! I'm waiting!
B: Just a minute. I'm coming as ______ as I can.
3 A: Did you lose at tennis again?
B: Yes, I played ______ and I lost.
4 A: Have you been working ______ today?
B: No, I've done nothing all day!
5 A: Have you finished that book yet?
B: No, I always read very ______ . It takes me a long time to finish a book.
6 A: Is he a bad student?
B: No, he does all his work very ______ .

D Put in the comparative adverb form of the adjective in brackets.

0 You must do your work _more carefully_ (careful) in future.
1 He has run the 100 metres ______ (fast) than any other athlete in the world this year.
2 Everyone else did the test ______ (good) than me.
3 You can travel ______ (cheap) at certain times of the year.
4 He plays ______ (confident) than he did in the past.
5 I'm sorry I've made so many mistakes. I'll try ______ (hard) in future.
6 You will be able to sit ______ (comfortable) in this chair.

41 Adverb + adjective (**very hot**); adjective + adjective; noun + noun (**a cardboard box**)

1

It was cold.

*It was **very** cold.*

We can use an adverb (e.g. **very**) before an adjective (e.g. **cold**) to make the adjective stronger. Some common adverbs we use in this way are:

very	**extremely**	**really**

*We were **very tired** after the trip.*
*I felt **extremely nervous** before the exam.*
*I'm **really angry** with you.* (= very angry)

We can also make an adjective weaker with these adverbs:

fairly	**quite**

*Our car is **fairly old**.*
(= It's old, but it isn't very old.)
*The meal was **quite nice**.*
(= It was nice but not wonderful.)

2 When we use two adjectives together, we order them like this:

- We use 'opinion' adjectives (e.g. **wonderful, nice, pleasant, strange**) before any other adjective (e.g. **new**):

	OPINION	
a	***wonderful,***	*new product*
a	***lovely,***	*warm day*
a	***beautiful,***	*little cottage*
a	***horrible,***	*green shirt*

- We use 'size' adjectives (e.g. **big, tall**) before an adjective that gives other information, for example its age (**new, old**), its colour, its shape (**thin, round**):

	SIZE	
a	***big,***	*new building*
a	***small,***	*red mark*
a	***huge,***	*black cloud*
a	***large,***	*round stone*

3 We can use two nouns together. The first noun is like an adjective and gives information about the second noun:

	NOUN	+ NOUN
a	*cardboard*	*box*
a	*cassette*	*recorder*
a	*cheque*	*book*
an	*alarm*	*clock*

Practice

A Complete these sentences using *really* or *quite*.

0 The film was __really__ good. I enjoyed it a lot.
1 It's __________ cold outside, but not very cold.
2 It isn't a wonderful book, but it's __________ good.
3 The tickets were __________ expensive – they cost much more than I expected.
4 This programme is __________ popular in my country; millions of people watch it.
5 He's __________ good at his job, but he sometimes makes bad mistakes.
6 The meal was __________ nice, but it wasn't very good.
7 It's __________ dangerous to drive so fast in such terrible weather conditions.
8 I'm not a very good tennis player, but I am __________ good.
9 They're all __________ intelligent students, and they will all pass their exams easily.
10 The company that I work for is __________ big, but it's not enormous.

B Put these words into the correct order.

0 (a – town – beautiful – little)
a beautiful, little town

1 (a – day – pleasant – sunny)
____

2 (a – smile – big – nice)
____

3 (a – large – coffee – black)
____

4 (a – old – coat – horrible)
____

5 (a – large – building – white)
____

6 (a – bird – big – grey)
____

7 (a – woman – thin – tall)
____

8 (a – small – car – blue)
____

9 (a – story – little – strange)
____

C Match the words in box A and box B to describe what you can see in each picture.

A				B			
	~~table~~	tennis	paper		cup	court	pot
	photograph	door	soup		handle	sign	hanger
	road	air	music		system	bowl	~~lamp~~
	coat	coffee	telephone		book	hostess	album

0 a table lamp

1 _______________

2 _______________

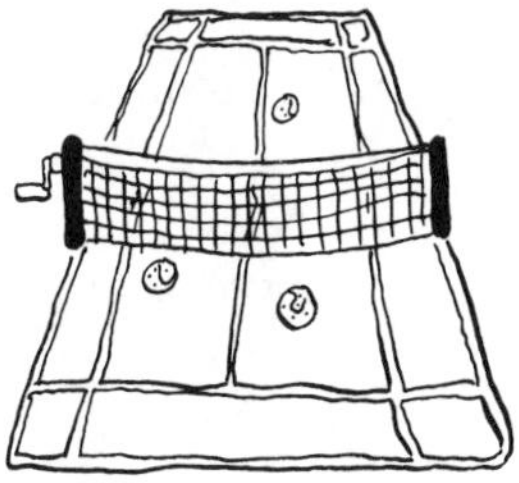
3 _______________

4 _______________

5 _______________

6 _______________

7 _______________

8 _______________

9 _______________

10 _______________

11 _______________

42 Prepositions of place and movement (**in**, **to** etc.)

1 We can use prepositions to talk about where things or people are. Look at the picture and the examples:

There is somebody ***in*** *the telephone box.*
There is a queue of people ***outside*** *the cinema.*
The people are standing ***on*** *the pavement.*
There is a clock ***above*** *the cinema entrance.*
The cinema entrance is ***under*** *the clock.*
The bank is ***next to*** *the cinema.*
The phone box is ***opposite*** *the cinema.*
The bank is ***between*** *the cinema and the café.*
There is a hill ***behind*** *the town.*
The car is ***in front of*** *the bank.*

2 We can also use prepositions to describe movement:

She walked ***out of*** *the house.*

I'm flying ***to*** *Italy tomorrow.*
I ran ***into*** *the station to catch the train.*

He jumped ***over*** *the wall.*

She walked ***under*** *the bridge.*

We walked ***through*** *the gate.*

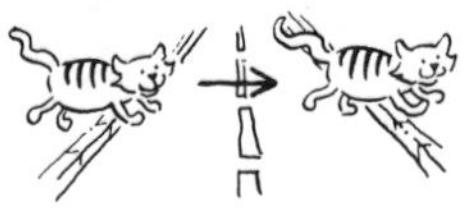

The cat ran ***across*** *the road.* (= from one side to the other side)

We walked ***along*** *the path.*

He ran ***up*** *the steps and knocked on the door.*
We cycled ***down*** *the hill.*

He ran ***between*** *two players and scored a goal.*

Practice

A **Look at the pictures and put in the correct prepositions in the sentences.**

0 
1 
2 
3 
4 

5 
6 
7 
8 
9 

0 The file is on ______ the desk.
1 She's sitting ______ her parents.
2 Do you like the picture ______ the door?
3 He was working ______ his office.
4 The car was parked ______ my house.
5 Where's the waste-paper basket? ~ It's ______ the desk.
6 The woman sitting ______ John on the plane was wearing a big hat.
7 The safe is ______ the picture.
8 They live ______ a caravan.
9 A young man with long hair was sitting ______ him.

B Put in the correct prepositions from the box. Use each preposition once.

under	to	through	down
between	~~along~~	out of	into
across	over	up	

0 She was walking along ______ the road that goes to the farm.
1 She swam ______ the pool from one side to the other.
2 We ran ______ the hill until we reached the bottom.
3 I climbed ______ the stairs to the top of the building.
4 The dog hid ______ the table, so that we couldn't see it.
5 I jumped ______ the sea and swam to the boat.
6 The horse jumped ______ the last fence and won the race.
7 The vase is ______ the photograph and the clock.
8 The rain came ______ the roof and into the house.
9 I walked ______ the house and went to my car.
10 I went ______ the shops and bought some food.

C Put in the correct words from the box. Use each word once.

behind	outside	in front of	out of	under
over	next to	on	~~into~~	through

0 He picked up the money and put it into ______ his pocket.
1 The man sitting ______ me was very tall and I couldn't see the game.
2 I keep a lot of useless things on the floor ______ the bed.
3 A fish jumped ______ the water and landed on the shore.
4 I always like to sit ______ the window on aeroplanes, so that I can look at the view.
5 Henry kicked the ball and it went ______ the window and into the kitchen.
6 He was standing ______ me, so I didn't see him.
7 The book that you're looking for is ______ the bottom shelf.
8 The ball went ______ my head, and I couldn't catch it.
9 The manager told me to wait ______ her office because she was talking to someone.

43 Prepositions: **in, with, by, without (by doing)**

1 We can use **in** to describe what somebody is wearing:

Jane is the woman ***in the red dress.***
I went to the interview ***in my new suit.***
It was a sunny day, and everyone was ***in summer clothes.***
Are you allowed to go to work ***in jeans?***
We saw some soldiers ***in uniform.***

2 We can use **with** to describe a part of somebody's body:

A small boy ***with red hair*** *came into the shop.*
Our teacher is a tall man ***with a beard.***
Lisa is a pretty girl ***with blue eyes.***
Jack was talking to a man ***with a big nose.***

We can also use **with** to describe animals:

A rabbit is an animal ***with big ears*** *and* ***a small tail.***

3 We can use **with** to talk about a part of something:

They live in a white house ***with a flat roof.***
I bought a shirt ***with red stripes.***
I used the pot ***with the wooden handle.***
He has a hi-fi ***with very big speakers.***

4 We can use **with** before something, for example a tool, that we use in order to do something:

You clean your teeth ***with a toothbrush.***
You open a tin ***with a tin opener.***
I cleaned the table ***with a cloth.***
Please eat ***with your knife*** *and* ***fork.***

5 We use **by** + **-ing** (e.g. **by doing**) to describe how we do or did something:

She learnt French ***by listening*** *to tapes.*
You start a car ***by turning*** *the key.*
She became successful in business ***by working*** *very hard.*
The prisoners escaped ***by climbing*** *over a wall.*

We use **without** + **-ing** (e.g. **without doing**) to say that a particular action is not done or was not done:

She passed the exam ***without doing*** *a lot of work.*
They left ***without waiting*** *for me.*
He did the work ***without making*** *any mistakes.*

Practice

A **Put in the correct prepositions. Use *in* or *with*.**

0 A young man with________ a moustache was driving the car.
1 He showed me a photograph of a woman ________ blue eyes.
2 We live in a house ________ a green door.
3 A lot of businessmen ________ suits were on the train.
4 There was a plant ________ big, green leaves in the corner of the room.
5 John was walking down the street with a woman ________ a black coat.
6 Look at that bull ________ those enormous horns!
7 One of the children was a girl ________ long, dark hair.
8 A man ________ a hat came into the café.
9 Soldiers ________ uniform were standing at the entrance to the building.
10 She wanted to buy a computer ________ a screen, a keyboard and a mouse.
11 We booked a hotel room ________ a bathroom.
12 It was cold, so I went out ________ a coat and scarf.
13 We've bought a television ________ a big screen.
14 He arrived for the meeting ________ a grey jacket.

B **Complete the sentences to describe which of the things in the box the people in the pictures are using.**

a spoon	a cloth	~~a brush~~
a broom	a racquet	a spade

0 

1 

2 

3 

4 

5 

0 She's painting with a brush.
1 He's digging ______________________
2 She's eating ______________________
3 You play tennis ______________________ and a ball.
4 He's sweeping the floor ______________________
5 She's cleaning the cooker ______________________

C **Rewrite each of the following using *by* or *without*.**

0 She sat in the corner. She didn't say anything.
She sat in the corner without saying anything.

0 He opened the door. He turned the key.
He opened the door by turning the key.

1 He repaired the car. He changed some of the parts.
____

2 She answered the question but she didn't read it carefully.
____

3 He left. He didn't say thank you.
____

4 She got the money because she sold her car.
____

5 I threw the letter away. I didn't open it.
____

6 We worked all day and we didn't eat anything.
____

7 He lost weight. He went on a strict diet.
____

8 I went out, but I didn't lock the door.
____

44 Relative clauses with **who, which** or **that**

1 Look at this example:
John married a woman.
John married a woman ***who works in his office.***
We can use **who** or **that** after a person (e.g. **woman**) to say who we are talking about. We call **who works in his office** a relative clause.

Here are some more examples:
Have you met Jackie? She's the girl ***that sits next to Mike in class.*** (Which girl? – The girl that sits next to Mike.)
I'm very friendly with the people ***who live downstairs.*** (Which people? – The people who live downstairs.)

2 If we are talking about a thing or an animal, we use **which** or **that**:
He took the job ***which paid the highest salary.*** (Which job? – The job which paid the highest salary.)
A kangaroo is an animal ***that lives in Australia.***

3 Notice that we do not say:
~~… *the people who* ***they*** *live downstairs*~~ .
~~… *an animal that* ***it*** *lives in Australia*~~ .

4 Look at this:

	SUBJECT	
Jane is the woman	*who*	*came for dinner.*
	She	came for dinner.

Here, **who** is the subject of the verb (**came**).

Now look at this:

	OBJECT	
Jackie is the girl	*who*	*you met last week.*
You met	her.	

Here, **who** is the object of the verb (**met**). We can also use **whom** instead of **who** as the object, but this is very unusual now in English:
She is the girl ***whom*** *you met.*

When **who, which** or **that** are the object, we can leave them out:
Jackie is the girl you met last week.

We do not use a pronoun (e.g. **her, them**) in addition to **who, which** or **that**:
~~*She is the girl* ***who*** *you met* ***her*** *last week.*~~

Practice

A **Join these sentences using *who* or *which*.**

0 We chose the hotel. It seemed to be the nicest.
We chose the hotel which seemed to be the nicest.

1 She spoke to the man. He was standing next to her.
____

2 I read the letters. They came in the morning post.
____

3 He likes the other people. They work in his office.
____

4 She's that singer. She was on television last night.
____

5 Next week there is a festival. It happens in the village every summer.
____

6 I paid the bills. They came yesterday.
____

B Complete the conversation by putting *who* or *which* into the gaps.

Carol: Did you watch that programme last night?

David: Which one?

Carol: The programme [0] which ______ I mentioned a couple of days ago. It's a new series [1] ______ started last night.

David: No, I didn't see it. Was it good?

Carol: Yes. It was about a group of friends [2] ______ were at school together. Well, Rupert . . .

David: Who was Rupert?

Carol: He was an old student of the school [3] ______ had become a doctor. He went to a party [4] ______ his old teachers organized. He met a lot of people [5] ______ had been at school with him many years before. They talked about the things [6] ______ they did when they were at school. Then suddenly, Rupert saw an old girl-friend [7] ______ was dancing with John …

David: Don't tell me any more. It's getting too complicated!

C Join these sentences using *who*, *which* or *that*, as in the example.

0 She chose the books. She wanted to buy them.
She chose the books that she wanted to buy.

1 We ate the sandwiches. Jack made them.
______

2 I'm doing some work. I have to finish it today.
______

3 She's an old woman. I often see her when I go to the shops.
______

4 He's an actor. A lot of people like him.
______

5 It's a magazine. I read it sometimes.
______

6 She was wearing a red dress. She wears for parties.
______

D Now join these sentences using *who* or *which*, as in the example.

0 The person phoned. He didn't leave a message.
The person who phoned didn't leave a message.

1 The bus goes to the airport. It leaves every 20 minutes.
______

2 The picture was hanging near the door. It was horrible.
______

3 The instructor taught me how to drive. He was very patient.
______

4 The girl was sitting next to me. She started talking to me.
______

Form tables

Table A Plural nouns

	SINGULAR	PLURAL
+ **-s** With most nouns we add **-s** to make them plural:	train suitcase radio	trains suitcases radios
+ **-es** With nouns that end with **-s**, **-ss**, **-sh**, **-ch**, **-x**, we add **-es**:	bus match box	buses matches boxes
-f/-fe → -ves We change **-f/-fe** to **-ves** in the plural:	loaf life	loaves lives
y → -ies With nouns that end with a consonant* + **-y**, we change the **-y** to **-ies:**	secretary city country	secretaries cities countries
Irregular nouns	man child foot	men children feet

Table B Present Simple

	I/you/we/they	**He/she/it**
+ **-s** After **he/she/it**, we add **-s** to most Present Simple verbs:	work leave use	works leaves uses
+ **-es** We add **-es** to verbs that end with **-ss**, **-sh**, **-ch**, **-o** (e.g. *finish*, *go*):	pass wash teach go do	passes washes teaches goes does
y → -ies We change **-y** to **-ies** with verbs that end with a consonant* + **-y**:	cry try fly	cries tries flies

* Consonants: b c d f g h j k l m n p q r s t v w x y z
Vowels: a e i o u
Syllables: | *hit* | = 1 syllable; | *vi* | *sit* | = 2 syllables; | *re* | *mem* | *ber* | = 3 syllables

Table C -ing forms

	INFINITIVE	-ing FORM
+ -**ing** With most verbs we add -**ing**:	walk read	walk**ing** read**ing**
~~e~~ + -**ing** With verbs that end with a consonant* + -**e**, we delete the -**e** and add -**ing**:	leave take make write	leav**ing** tak**ing** mak**ing** writ**ing**
ie → -ying With verbs that end with -**ie**, we change -**ie** to -**ying**:	lie die	l**ying** d**ying**
-t → -tting With verbs that end with one vowel* + one consonant (e.g. ***sit***, ***hit***, ***shop***), we double the consonant:	**get** **run** shop	ge**tting** ru**nning** sho**pping**
+ -**ing** But note that we do not double the consonant, (1) when it is a **y** or **w** (e.g. *play*), (2) when the last syllable* is not stressed (e.g. *reMEMber, VISit*):	play snow remember visit listen	play**ing** snow**ing** remember**ing** visit**ing** listen**ing**

Table D Regular verbs: Past Simple and past participle

	INFINITIVE	PAST SIMPLE	PAST PARTICIPLE
+ -**ed** With most verbs we add -**ed**:	enjoy finish	enjoy**ed** finish**ed**	enjoy**ed** finish**ed**
+ -**d** With verbs ending with -**e**, we add -**d**:	close phone	close**d** phone**d**	close**d** phone**d**
y → -ied With verbs that end with a consonant* + -**y**, we change the **y** to -**ied**:	carry marry	carr**ied** marr**ied**	carr**ied** marr**ied**
p → -pped With verbs that end with one vowel* + one consonant (e.g. ***stop***), we double the consonant:	stop plan	sto**pped** pla**nned**	sto**pped** pla**nned**
+ -**ed** But note that we do not double the consonant, (1) when it is a **y** or **w** (e.g. *stay*), (2) when the last syllable* is not stressed (e.g. *LISten, HAppen, Open*):	stay listen happen open visit	stay**ed** listen**ed** happen**ed** open**ed** visit**ed**	stay**ed** listen**ed** happen**ed** open**ed** visit**ed**

* Consonants: b c d f g h j k l m n p q r s t v w x y z
Vowels: a e i o u
Syllables: | *hit* | = 1 syllable; | *vi* | *sit* | = 2 syllables; | *re* | *mem* | *ber* | = 3 syllables

Table E Irregular verbs: Past Simple and past participle

INFINITIVE	PAST SIMPLE	PAST PARTICIPLE
be	was/were	been
become	became	become
begin	began	begun
break	broke	broken
bring	brought	brought
build	built	built
buy	bought	bought
catch	caught	caught
choose	chose	chosen
come	came	come
cost	cost	cost
cut	cut	cut
do	did	done
drink	drank	drunk
drive	drove	driven
eat	ate	eaten
fall	fell	fallen
feel	felt	felt
find	found	found
fly	flew	flown
forget	forgot	forgotten
get	got	got
give	gave	given
go	went	gone
grow	grew	grown
have	had	had
hear	heard	heard
hide	hid	hidden
hit	hit	hit
hold	held	held
hurt	hurt	hurt
keep	kept	kept
know	knew	known
learn	learnt/learned	learnt/learned
leave	left	left

INFINITIVE	PAST SIMPLE	PAST PARTICIPLE
lend	lent	lent
let	let	let
lose	lost	lost
make	made	made
meet	met	met
pay	paid	paid
put	put	put
read	read	read
ring	rang	rung
run	ran	run
say	said	said
see	saw	seen
sell	sold	sold
send	sent	sent
show	showed	shown/showed
shut	shut	shut
sing	sang	sung
sit	sat	sat
sleep	slept	slept
speak	spoke	spoken
spell	spelt/spelled	spelt/spelled
spend	spent	spent
stand	stood	stood
steal	stole	stolen
swim	swam	swum
take	took	taken
teach	taught	taught
tell	told	told
think	thought	thought
throw	threw	thrown
understand	understood	understood
wake	woke	woken
wear	wore	worn
win	won	won
write	wrote	written

Table F Comparative and superlative adjectives

	ADJECTIVE	COMPARATIVE	SUPERLATIVE
+ -er/-est We add **-er /-est** to short adjectives (one-syllable* adjectives):	warm tall young	warm**er** tall**er** young**er**	the warm**est** the tall**est** the young**est**
+ -r/-st **We** add **-r/-st** to adjectives that end with **-e**:	late	late**r**	the late**st**
-g → -gger With short adjectives that end with one vowel* and one consonant* (e.g. ***big***), we double the consonant:	**big** **hot** **wet**	**bigger** **hotter** **wetter**	the **biggest** the **hottest** the **wettest**
-w + -er /-est We don't double **w**:	low	low**er**	the low**est**
more/most We use **more / the most** before adjectives of two or more syllables*:	expensive famous beautiful	**more** expensive **more** famous **more** beautiful	the **most** expensive the **most** famous the **most** beautiful
y → -ier/-iest But note that with adjectives ending with **-y** (e.g. ***happy***), we change **-y** to **-ier /-iest**:	happy lucky easy	happ**ier** luck**ier** eas**ier**	the happ**iest** the luck**iest** the eas**iest**
Irregular adjectives:	good bad far	better worse farther	the best the worst the farthest

Table G Adverbs

	ADJECTIVE	ADVERB
+ -ly With most adverbs, we add **-ly** to the adjective:	quick correct slow	quick**ly** correct**ly** slow**ly**
Exceptions: Adjectives that end with **-y** (**y → -ily**):	 happy lucky	 happ**ily** luck**ily**
Adjectives that end with **-ble** (~~-e~~ + **y**):	remarka**ble**	remarka**bly**
Irregular adverbs	good fast hard late	well fast hard late

* Consonants: b c d f g h j k l m n p q r s t v w x y z
Vowels: a e i o u
Syllables: | *hit* | = 1 syllable; | *vi* | *sit* | = 2 syllables; | *re* | *mem* | *ber* | = 3 syllables

Exit tests

You can do these tests when you have finished studying the units in this book, to see if there are units that you should look at again. In the tests, each question relates to the unit with the same number, e.g. question 1 tests something from unit 1, question 2 tests something from unit 2, etc.

Exit test 1

Choose the right answer (**a**, **b**, or **c**) and write **a**, **b**, or **c** in the box, as in the example.

0 Where **a** do **b** does **c** is John live? *b*

1 Ann **a** finishs **b** finish **c** finishes work at 6 o'clock. ☐

2 I **a** am makeing **b** making **c** 'm making an omelette. ☐

3 Diana **a** is doing **b** does **c** do a French course at the moment. ☐

4 We **a** staied **b** stayyed **c** stayed in a nice hotel last weekend. ☐

5 He **a** was cook **b** did cooking **c** was cooking a meal when I arrived. ☐

6 I **a** know **b** 've known **c** am knowing Julia for many years. ☐

7 A parcel **a** just has arrived **b** has arrived yet **c** has just arrived for you. ☐

8 We **a** 've arrived **b** arrived **c** have arrive at the hotel late last night. ☐

9 I **a** live **b** 've been living **c** 'm living here for ten years. ☐

10 I knew her name because I **a** had meet **b** was met **c** had met her before. ☐

11 I **a** 'll take **b** going to take **c** 'll to take you to the airport. ☐

12 Joan **a** is starting **b** start **c** is start her new job next week. ☐

13 If you **a** 'll leave **b** leave **c** are leaving soon, you'll catch the 11 o'clock bus. ☐

14 I **a** ask **b** 'll ask **c** am asking him to phone you, when he gets home. ☐

15 I like this kind of music. ~ **a** So do I. **b** I like, too. **c** So am I. ☐

16 Alison never **a** listens **b** listens to **c** listens at the radio. ☐

17 I often **a** do **b** get **c** make mistakes when I'm typing. ☐

18 We **a** arrived here yesterday. **b** here arrived yesterday. **c** yesterday arrived here. ☐

19 Who **a** went **b** did go **c** did they go to the party last night? ☐

20 How **a** far **b** long **c** much is it from here to your office? ~ About 2 kilometres. ☐

21 You come from Scotland, **a** don't you? **b** isn't it? **c** are you? ☐

22 Excuse me. I **a** must make **b** must I make **c** must to make a phone call. ☐

23 She **a** has work **b** have to work **c** has to work very hard in her job. ☐

24 You **a** shouldn't eat **b** shouldn't to eat **c** don't should eat so quickly. ☐

25 I **a** couldn't to hear **b** didn't could hear **c** couldn't hear what the man said. ☐

26 This article **a** wrote **b** was written **c** written by a famous journalist. ☐

27 Margaret enjoys **a** learning **b** to learn **c** learn languages. ☐

28 Alan wants **a** work **b** working **c** to work abroad in the future. ☐

29 He said that he **a** post **b** would post **c** will post the letter yesterday. ☐

30 Louise works in **a** the **b** — **c** a shop in New York, but I don't know its name. ☐

31 Mary put a bandage on Tom's finger, because he cut **a** herself **b** him **c** himself when he was preparing the meal. ☐

32 The man **a** offered me **b** to me offered **c** me offered a cigarette. ☐

33 I don't know **a** nothing **b** something **c** anything about the history of Britain. ☐

34 I was at home **a** all day **b** all the day **c** all of day yesterday. ☐

35 I've met **a** both of **b** both the **c** either of her parents and I like them. ☐

36 Frank is **a** taller as **b** taller than **c** more tall than me. ☐

37 My job is **a** as difficult as **b** difficult as **c** as difficult that your job. ☐

38 I didn't go into the museum because it was **a** too expensive. **b** too much expensive. **c** expensive enough. ☐

39 John **a** doesn't interest **b** isn't interested **c** isn't interesting in art. ☐

40 She read the letter **a** careful. **b** carefuly. **c** carefully. ☐

41 I asked for a **a** small, white coffee. **b** coffee small, white. **c** white, small coffee. ☐

42 He walked **a** across **b** through **c** along the road to the other side of the street. ☐

43 She was wearing a T-shirt **a** in **b** by **c** with a red and blue pattern. ☐

44 I stayed with a friend **a** who she lives **b** who lives **c** which lives in the city. ☐

Total: ☐ / 44

Exit test 2

Choose the right answer (**a**, **b**, **c**) and write **a**, **b**, or **c** in the box, as in the example.

0 Who **a** is **b** do **c** did Jane meet? [c]

1 Jane **a** don't like **b** doesn't likes **c** doesn't like burgers. [ ]

2 Carol **a** is writeing **b** is writting **c** is writing a postcard. [ ]

3 Lessons **a** are starting **b** start **c** are start at 9 o'clock every morning. [ ]

4 The letter **a** came not **b** didn't came **c** didn't come yesterday. [ ]

5 Her parents **a** weren't waiting **b** didn't wait **c** wasn't waiting for her when she arrived at the airport. [ ]

6 I **a** have visitted **b** 've visit **c** 've visited Africa several times. [ ]

7 The post **a** hasn't arrived yet. **b** already hasn't arrived. **c** yet hasn't arrived. [ ]

8 He's a good friend of mine. I **a** have known **b** knew **c** know him for ten years. [ ]

9 Lisa has been learning English **a** for **b** since **c** from two years. [ ]

10 When I arrived at the station, the train **a** had left. **b** has left. **c** was left. [ ]

11 Which film **a** do you go to see **b** you will see **c** are you going to see tonight? [ ]

12 When **a** you moving **b** are you moving **c** move you to your new home? [ ]

13 You **a** don't have **b** aren't having **c** won't have any money left if you buy that suit. [ ]

14 When Mary **a** will get **b** gets **c** is getting here, we'll go out. [ ]

15 Michael doesn't speak French and **a** his brother neither. **b** neither does his brother. **c** neither his brother. [ ]

16 We **a** reached to **b** reached at **c** reached home at 3 a.m. [ ]

17 Tina **a** had **b** got **c** made very angry with me. [ ]

18 When **a** did you visit China? **b** did you China visit? **c** you did visit China? [ ]

19 What **a** you saw **b** saw you **c** did you see in Madrid? [ ]

20 Susan **a** has 19 years. **b** is 19. **c** has 19. [ ]

21 I've met you before, **a** didn't I? **b** did I? **c** haven't I? [ ]

22 I **a** mustn't spend **b** don't must spend **c** must not to spend any more money today. [ ]

23 I **a** haven't to get up **b** don't have to get up **c** have not get up early tomorrow, because I'm on holiday. [ ]

24 Which bus **a** I should catch? **b** should I to catch? **c** should I catch? ☐

25 I **a** might not go **b** don't might go **c** mightn't to go to the meeting tomorrow. ☐

26 The robber **a** was seen **b** had seen **c** saw by a policeman. ☐

27 I **a** like to go **b** would like to go **c** like going to the cinema tonight. ☐

28 John didn't have a pen, so I let **a** him to borrow **b** him borrow **c** that he borrowed mine. ☐

29 Susan **a** told **b** said me **c** told me that she had enjoyed her holiday. ☐

30 Stuart is a vegetarian. He doesn't eat **a** — **b** the **c** a meat. ☐

31 We enjoyed **a** ourselves **b** us **c** ourself a lot on our holiday. ☐

32 A friend **a** to me lent **b** me lent **c** lent me some money. ☐

33 I'm hungry because I haven't eaten **a** anything **b** nothing **c** something all day. ☐

34 **a** None of **b** None of the **c** None shops were open, so we couldn't buy any food. ☐

35 She asked Mark and Trudy, but they couldn't help her because **a** either of **b** neither of **c** both them knew the answer. ☐

36 He is **a** best **b** the best **c** the better player in the team. ☐

37 I haven't visited **a** as many countries than **b** as much countries as **c** as many countries as you have. ☐

38 We couldn't go into the museum because we didn't have **a** money enough. **b** too many money. **c** enough money. ☐

39 There is nothing to do in this town. I'm **a** bored. **b** bore. **c** boring. ☐

40 Linda speaks Spanish **a** better as **b** better than **c** best than I do. ☐

41 I work in a **a** modern, tall building. **b** tall, modern building. **c** building tall modern. ☐

42 They climbed **a** over **b** in **c** between the wall and landed on the other side. ☐

43 We drove 300 kilometres without **a** stop. **b** stopping. **c** to stop. ☐

44 This is the book **a** that we used **b** which did we use **c** which we used it on the course. ☐

Total: ☐ / 44

Index

The numbers in the index are unit numbers. They are not page numbers.